The Climber's Guide to
North America

The Climber's Guide to North America

Volume II
Rocky Mountain Rock Climbs

by

John Harlin, III

illustrations by Adele Hammond

CHOCKSTONE PRESS

Denver, Colorado
1985

Published by
Chockstone Press
526 Franklin Street
Denver, Colorado 80218

Distributed in Great Britain and Europe by
Cordee, Ltd.
3a DeMontfort St.
Leicester
LE1 7HD
Great Britain

Printed in the United States of America

Library of Congress Cataloging in Publication Data
Harlin, John, 1956-
    Rocky Mountain rock climbs

    (The climber's guide to North America ; v. 2)
    Includes index
    1. Rock climbing--Rocky Mountains--Guide-books.
2. Rocky Mountains--Guide-books.   I. Title.
II. Series: Harlin, John, 1956-   .   Climber's guide
to North America ; v. 2.
GV199.44.R59H37   1985   917   85-9669
ISBN 0-9609452-8-8

ISBN 0-9609452-8-8 (Rocky Mountain Rock Climbs)
ISBN 0-9609452-5-3 (Climber's Guide to North America—full series)

ACKNOWLEDGEMENTS

A number of people have helped to make this book possible. The list below is of those who have made important contributions. If I have inadvertently forgotten someone, my most sincere apologies are hereby extended.

The following people have made an extra effort to help me with this book. The hours and sometimes days that they have put in have made this a far better book than it would have been without their help. Were I not so lazy, I would give them all the individualized acknowledgements they deserve.

Bob Archbold, Stacy and Mark Austin, Dave Bingham, Chip Chace, Leonard Coyne, Dick DuMais, Nichols J. Eason: Canyonlands National Park, Adele Hammond, Arno Ilgner, Dave Jones, Mark J. Kelleher, Kurt Kleiner, Steve Komito, Layne Kopischka, Ron Olevsky, Pat Parmenter, Paul Piana, Glenn Randall, Roger Rudolph: Zion National Park, Antoine Savelli, Lee Sheftel.

These people have either supplied me with photographs or helped in various ways to make this a better book.

David M. Benyak, Doug Couleur, Reid Dowdle, Chester Dreiman, Mike Engle, Pat Ellinwood, Charlie Fowler, Nuriel Guedalia, Gary Gray, Dan Hare, Ann Hayes, Mike Hill, Steve Hong, Dennis Horning, Jim Howe, Mark Jacobs, Glen Kaye: Rocky Mountain National Park, Bill Kees, Cito Kirkpatrick, Gregg Lindsay, Alex Lowe, Jeff Lowe, Kent Lugbill, R. Kim Miller, Vern Phinney, Mark Pey, Adele Smith, Carl W. Smith, Hidetaka and Michiko Suzuki, Ken Trout, Ed Webster, Billy Westbay, and Ted Wilson.

ENVIRONMENTAL IMPACT

While this guide may reduce the environmental impact on certai popular climbing areas, it will cause increased strain on others. T alleviate this stress, climbers are strongly urged to respect the individua character of each area that they visit.

Many people can be absorbed into a wilderness and still maintain quality experience if one basic rule is followed: minimize your impac Shouting, including belay signals, should be reduced or eliminatec Camping, if out of designated sites, should be kept as discreet as possible above all, nothing should be left behind that leaves any indication tha you have been there.

Littering is unthinkable in the outdoors. This includes not just sca tered garbage, but also unburied excrement, new fire-rings, and dishe washed in lakes and streams.

People who are disrespectful of the environment should be tactfull educated about the consequences of their actions. In addition, we shoul pick up after those who defile our communal space. This demonstratio of love for the environment is the best educational eye-opener. It als means that we don't have to endure that particular piece of litter mor than once.

TABLE OF CONTENTS

INTRODUCTION

Charlie Fowler on 7 Arrows — RMNP

THE CLIMBER'S GUIDE TO NORTH AMERICA

'or many years, the imagination of most climbers could be caught by
)nly a few famous cliffs and mountains. But as the sport grew in
)opularity, climbers began searching out unheralded areas—places where
hey could explore new territory and leave behind some of the increasing
:rowds. Soon, they discovered that North America holds a great diversity
)f climbing areas, each unique in its climbing experience.

This series of guides was conceived to provide an efficient sampling
)f many different North American climbing areas. Based primarily on
)hotographs, the books also offer selected route descriptions, access
naps, and background information for each covered area. *The Climber's
;uide to North America* will allow travelling climbers to experience for
hemselves the special character of these places through several days of
:xcellent climbing.

AREA SELECTION

The areas for this volume are chosen with the following criteria: the
limbing must be accessible by moderate hiking from a car-camping
)asecamp, and it must be interesting enough to make it worth either a
pecial trip or a brief stop for climbers on their way elsewhere. In
ddition, the popularity and quality of the area has generally gained it
1ational or international attention.

Because some people deeply resent the popularization of their favorite
1aunts—fearing that publicity will spoil the original environment and
tmosphere—climbers are urged to respect the individual character of
he place they are visiting. It is especially important to minimize one's
mpact on the environment.

The many areas not included in this book will remain a bit mysterious
nd wild. Eventually, some of these may be opened to the public through
uidebooks or magazine articles, but it is not for this book to do so
)rematurely.

SELECTION OF ROUTES

A sufficient number of routes have been included to provide a good
ampling of the climbing in each area. Depending on the size of the
rea, this will vary from several days' to a couple of weeks' worth of

climbing. Routes are included in the most popular difficulty range: from 5.6 to 5.12.

While the routes included are intended to represent the better routes at an area, not all will be considered "classic." Sometimes, especially in the lower grades, lesser routes were included in the book in order to provide climbing at a particular level. Some classic routes may not be included because of layout considerations.

HOW TO USE THIS BOOK
Each chapter has the same format. Photographs and route information follow a written description of each area, including the nature of the climbing and environment. Below is a more detailed explanation of how to interpret each chapter.

HIGHLIGHTS This is a one paragraph overview of the characteristics of the area.

CLIMBING This section comments on the different cliffs, the type of rock, the nature of climbing (whether it be face, crack, slab, free, or aid), the approach hikes, and descents.

ENVIRONMENT The natural and social environment described in this paragraph gives a feeling for the area. The climbing experience can, of course, vary from wilderness, to that of a crowded climber's gymnasium. This section will also mention some alternate attractions that the area offers, including hikes, scenery, and river rafting.

CLIMBING HISTORY A brief overview of the local climbing history is presented in this section. Individual names have been omitted, however, because in such a brief treatment it is difficult to properly recognize those people who have contributed to the development of an area. The important names can often, though not always, be garnered from the first ascent list. Local guidebooks will sometimes help considerably in providing a more in-depth historical overview.

CAMPING A description of the availability and nature of camping (legal), showering, and laundry facilities is covered here. Free illegal or discretionary camping can often be found, but such information cannot be put in this book. Because prices are likely to increase through the years, treat the specific dollar figures as approximations. Up to six people are typically allowed per site, in one or sometimes two vehicles. As mentioned in A NOTE ON SAFETY, lake and stream water can rarely be trusted for drinking. To protect the water, toilets should be used where available, or excrement should be buried not less than 100 feet from any stream or lake. A biodegradable soap should also be used.

SEASONS AND WEATHER This is a general chart of the seasonal weather and likelihood of finding good climbing days. Temperatures are given by ten degree intervals with a plus (+) or minus (−) sign designating that temperatures are frequently found either above or below this range. Thus, 70's indicates that temperatures are typically somewhere between seventy and eighty degrees Fahrenheit. 70's+ indicates that the temperature frequently reaches into the eighties. 70's− indicates that often the temperature never reaches seventy degrees. The column "High" is for the typical highest daytime temperature, while "Low" is for the typical overnight lowest temperature. "Likelihood of Precipitation" gives a clue to whether the visitor will encounter rain or snow that will inhibit climbing.

"Frequency of Climbable Days" is a summation of the temperature and precipitation data and some of the "Comments" listed below the chart. It is the best indicator of whether moderate climbers will be able to enjoy themselves during a visit. If an area indicates "low-medium" frequency of climbable days, then a short visit might typically be rained out or the temperatures might be too high or low. A longer visit would probably yield at least a few days to climb in. Of course, zealots will find climbing possible even on hot or wet days.

These charts, based as they are on weather average data, are as variable as any weather.

RESTRICTIONS AND WARNINGS Some of the listings here, such as whether one may encounter rattlesnakes, or thieves, are for the reader's personal benefit. More important is such advice as "go slowly through the residential area" because this information is necessary for maintaining access privileges for the entire climbing community. PLEASE READ AND HEED THIS SECTION!

GUIDEBOOKS This section lists the local guidebooks and how to obtain them. A climber on an extended visit may require information for additional routes beyond those provided in this book. In addition, a local guidebook can be invaluable for more information on the area's history and geology.

GUIDE SERVICES AND EQUIPMENT STORES Local equipment stores can be a good source of updated information. The locally based guide services are listed for those in need of either instruction or a well qualified partner.

EMERGENCY SERVICES The nearest hospital, and the appropriate contact for rescues is described here. In virtually all cases, the County Sheriff is in charge of coordinating rescues (except in National Parks where the rangers are responsible). Because telephone numbers can change, simply call the operator to make the connection. Rescues should be called only in case of dire emergencies. Not only does this save the climber and the taxpayer a great deal of money, but self-rescue does not generate the ill-will towards the climbing community that often is the result of very public rescues. A European-style climber's rescue insurance policy is not yet available in North America.

GETTING THERE This section describes the public transportation available to the climbing area.

ROUTE DESCRIPTIONS
Most of the route descriptions in this book follow a series of dots placed directly onto photographs. Difficulty, fixed protection, and belay notations are written next to the route lines. As noted repeatedly in this introduction, this is only a guide. The lines on the photographs are approximate in their placement and route finding skills are a necessity.
On many longer climbs, supplementary drawings—"topos"—are also included. The following drawing explains the symbolism used.Suggested protection is only given when it differs from the standard rack most climbers usually carry with them. In the case of free climbs, assume that the listed protection is in addition to a clean (no pitons) rack with one nut from each of the standard size increments from one quarter inch to two and one-half inches.

INTRODUCTION 5

Unless they are listed in the guidebook, or needed in emergency situations, PITONS OR BOLTS SHOULD NEVER BE PLACED ON ESTABLISHED NORTH AMERICAN ROUTES!

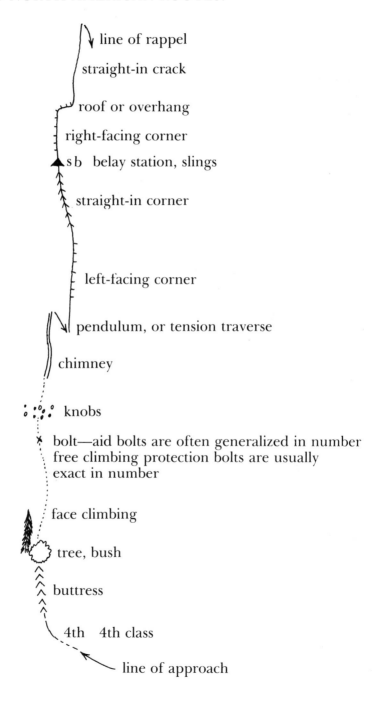

line of rappel

straight-in crack

roof or overhang

right-facing corner

s b belay station, slings

straight-in corner

left-facing corner

pendulum, or tension traverse

chimney

knobs

bolt—aid bolts are often generalized in number free climbing protection bolts are usually exact in number

face climbing

tree, bush

buttress

4th   4th class

line of approach

fp	fixed piton
lb	lieback
sb	sling belay
ow	offwidth
chim	chimney
thin	thin crack
165'	165 feet
KB	knifeblade piton
LA	Lost Arrow piton

Key to the Maps

freeway	▬▬▬▬▬
paved road	———————
unpaved road	– – – – —
trail	· · · · · · · · · · ·
camping	Δ
area location or summit	★
mile	mi.

RATINGS

North American climbers use a combination of four rating systems for assessing the difficulty of climbs. The first is a rough classification that distinguishes between the various stages from trail hiking to aid climbing. The next system breaks the technical free climbing category down into much more specific ratings. This Decimal System (widely referred to as the Yosemite Decimal System—YDS—but actually developed at Tahquitz) is the mainstay of rock climbing route ratings. These free ratings refer to the hardest individual moves on a particular section of rock. Sometimes an overall route rating will be raised some if the climbing is extremely continuous, but this practice is not universal. Rarely lack of protection affect the free rating of a climb; instead, protection considerations are mentioned more as a footnote to the grade. Aid climbing is also differentiated into various degrees of difficulty; seriousness is a part of the rating.

Many routes are additionally given a roman numeral grade to indicate their length. Thus, an example of an overall route rating might be VI 5.10 A3. Individual pitches might be labelled 5.6, 4th, or A2. An explanation of each category follows.

CLASS DESCRIPTION

1	Trail hiking
2	Rough hiking, frequent use of hands for balance
3rd	Rock scrambling using hands, sometimes with enough exposure that inexperienced climbers will prefer to use a rope
4th	Technically more difficult and sufficiently exposed that most climbers use a rope and belay for safety
5th	Free climbing sufficiently difficult to require the use of a rope and placement of protection for safety
6th	Artificial (aid) climbing where hardware is used not simply for protection, but also for hand and footholds

5th class climbing is subdivided by the use of a decimal point. Thus routes are rated 5.0, 5.1, . . . 5.11, 5.12. Currently the most difficult climbs are in the 5.13 category. Routes 5.10 or greater in difficulty usually receive further subgradings in the form of letters (a, b, c, or d) or + and − signs. The following is an approximate comparison of the most popular rating systems used throughout the world.

Decimal	UIAA	English Numerical	Australian	French
5.0	III		4	
5.1	III +		5	
5.2	IV −	3a	6	
5.3		3b	7	
5.4	IV +	3c	8,9	
5.5	V −	4a	10,11	
5.6	V	4b	12,13	4c
5.7	V +	4c	14,15	5a
5.8	VI −	5a	16	5b
5.9	VI		17	5c
5.10a (−)	VI +	5b	18	6a
5.10b	VII −		19	
5.10c (+)	VII	5c	20	6b
5.10d	VII +		21	
5.11a (−)		6a	22	6c
5.11b	VIII −		23	
5.11c (+)	VIII	6b	24	7a
5.11d	VIII +		25	
5.12a (−)	IX −	6c	26	7b
5.12b	IX		27	
5.12c (+)	IX +	7a	28	7c
5.12d			29	
5.13	X	7b		

The aid ratings reflect the security of using the latest available technology. The same route climbed with the pitons of the 1960's instead of the modern aid climbing rack would require entirely different ratings. Frequently, difficult modern routes could not be done without the technology of Friends, bashies and hooks.

A1 Easy placements, completely secure.

A2 More difficult placements, less secure.

A3 Even more difficult placements that will usually only hold a short fall.

A4 Each placement will hold body weight but would not sustain a fall.

A5 A series of A4 placements long enough to risk at least a 50 foot fall should one fail.

C1, C2, ... are used as an aid rating prefix, where known, to indicate the aid rating when the route can be done completely clean—i.e., with no hammer blows.

Roman numerals, intended as a grading of overall difficulty, were designed to reflect many factors about a route, including commitment, difficulty, and length. In current usage, they primarily reflect length in terms of time invested into a climb.

I About an hour of climbing, usually one or two pitches.

II Less than a half day of climbing.

III A half day of climbing.

IV A full day of climbing.

V Typically, one overnight is spent on the wall. Since many traditional two-day aid routes are free climbed in a day, this grade on a free climb usually means one very long day.

VI At least two nights are usually spent on the climb.

WARNING ON ROUTE LINES, SYMBOLS, AND FIXED PROTECTION

The format taken for most of the route descriptions in this book—route lines superimposed on photographs—is helpful only if one keeps in mind the inherent imprecision of route information. In this book, the placement of route lines or protection/belay symbols is not exact. The notations are subject to interpretation, and route finding skills are just as important as ever. The symbols and route lines are guides only.

There are bound to be ways to improve the accuracy of the route line drawings or topos in this book. While any guidebook takes away some of the adventure in climbing, it is not the intent of this guide to mislead. As a user of this guide, your suggestions for better descriptions would be invaluable. A photocopy of a photo with corrections to the route line is ideal. Likewise, feedback concerning the routes selected for this book is appreciated. Suggestions for better routes are welcomed. All route information, corrections and suggestions should be sent to Chockstone Press, 526 Franklin Street, Denver, CO 80218.

As further warning, be aware that fixed pitons and bolts labelled in this guide might have been removed or supplemented. Fixed anchors should always be carefully inspected. They may be weak due to weathering, poor initial placement, or any number of reasons. That they are listed in this book does not imply that they are trustworthy or even exist! Where not considered necessary for route finding, known fixed pitons or bolts have often been left out of the route description.

Pitons should not be trusted without testing, preferably with a hammer. Since few climbers free climb with a hammer, fixed pitons are rarely tested and can easily be unsafe.

Bolts should be checked with a strong jerk on the hanger (using a carabiner) and inspected for cracks.They should NEVER be tested with a hammer, as this can severely weaken them! Because defective or poorly placed bolts are a possibility anywhere, no bolt can be fully trusted.

A NOTE ON SAFETY

Those using *The Climber's Guide to North America* as a guidebook are assumed to be competent and experienced climbers. It is not the intent of this book to educate anyone in HOW to climb, but simply to provide suggestions as to where to climb and what it will be like.

It must be noted, however, that many of the places covered by these books are relatively remote. Assistance from fellow climbers, rescues, or hospital facilities may be difficult to obtain quickly.This is a serious consideration that should be taken into account when deciding just how far to "hang it out" on a particular climb.

Water sanitation can be a problem in some areas. Beware that few streams and lakes can be completely trusted to be safe from contamination—no matter how far away from "civilization." The bacteria Giardia is a common infectious agent and can produce extreme intestinal ills that can completely ruin a climbing vacation. It is best to thoroughly boil and/or treat with purification tablets all stream and lake water.

To avoid further water contamination, all human waste should be buried not less than 100 feet away from the nearest open water.

Theft can be a definite problem in some areas, particularly those with large numbers of people. As a general rule, keep all valuables, including climbing equipment, locked out of sight in a car. Ropes and equipment fixed on routes, or stashed at the base of cliffs, may not be safe.

IF YOU DON'T HAVE A CAR

Public transportation in North America is not nearly as extensive as it is in Europe. Nevertheless, one can certainly reach many of the best climbing areas on the continent without a car. If the climber is willing to hitch-hike, there is almost no place that cannot be reached. Though trains bypass almost everything interesting to climbers, buses connect the major cities with most small communities and some popular recreation sites. From the major airports, it is usually necessary to take a connecting bus to the bus station located downtown.

If you don't have a car, turn to the text under *GETTING THERE* for the area you are interested in visiting. A valuable further reference is the book *How to Get to the Wilderness Without a Car* listed under *SUPPLEMENTARY INFORMATION* in this book.

Another option is to rent a car. The major car rental companies found at airports are fairly expensive. The same rental agencies located do vn-town often offer considerably lower rates. Much cheaper, though ris' ier, alternatives are the small local companies that rent used cars—sometimes VERY used. By getting together a small group of climbers one of these cars can be rented for very little money and will provide a great deal of mobility. Likewise, even climbers with limited resources can usually afford to buy a suitable used car by pooling their funds. An important fringe benefit to having a car is that the trunk provides a storage place for gear.

If travelling alone or with one other person, consider first visiting one of the more popular areas. There is a good possibility of meeting a climber with a car who can be persuaded to visit new places.

AMERICAN ROCK CLIMBING STYLE AND ETHICS

Traditionally, there has been a difference in free climbing attitudes between Europe and America. These stem in large part from the fact that Europeans have emphasized getting up big mountains fast (crag climbing was often considered practice for the real stuff). Popular American cliffs are low in objective dangers, thus Americans have emphasized the style of the ascent. Now, many Europeans are also concentrating on pure rock climbing and have adopted many similar standards of style. Nevertheless, a short discussion on American attitudes may help visitors from different climbing cultures.

In the United States, the ideal free ascent is a route climbed unpre-viewed, unroped, barefoot, and without chalk. Any compromise of this style is just that: a compromise. To provide a greater margin of safety and comfort, few climbers follow such strict guidelines in their climbing style. Many climbers use chalk, most use shoes, and almost everyone uses a rope and protection. They strive simply to climb a route with the minimum number of falls or reliances on equipment, knowing that the further that their style deviates from the ideal, the less the accomplish-ment of their ascent.

There are many ways of compromising good climbing style, from merely falling, to resting on protection, yo-yoing (making upward prog-ress by lowering to rest, or exchanging leaders), previewing the route by rappel, or pre-placing protection. "Improving" hand or footholds by altering the rock is unthinkable.

Some Europeans consider it good style to practice a route by resting on aid with the intent of finally re-leading the route with no weighting of protection. Most Americans would rather complete the route in one push using their best possible style, even if it means taking falls and lowering to a rest position. Many people prefer to retreat from a short route than to ever rest on aid.

Damaging the rock is the biggest transgression in American rock climbing. Because of their damaging impact on the rock, the use of pitons is discouraged on all free climbs and wherever avoidable on aid routes. On first ascents, any necessary pitons are usually left fixed. The use of bolts on established routes is even more deeply scorned. On the free climbs described in this book, both pitons and bolts should be thought of only as emergency tools.

Chalk is disapproved of by many climbers—both because it is an aid and because it is visually obnoxious on some rock types. It also leaves a "white-dotted line" that shows where to go and where all the hand-holds are. Nevertheless, the stuff works wonderfully in securing grip and is used by most climbers.

Discussions on ethics and style are taken quite seriously by many people. Generally these discussions center on first ascents, because a route that is put up in poor style can take away the thrill and credit for first ascent by someone who would later do the route in a more accepted style.

Many Americans will be seen bending the "rules" of good style, but when all is said and done, most climbing peers condemn only those who 1) damage the rock, 2) misrepresent their particular climbing style, or 3) grossly deny other climbers a first ascent in better style.

SUPPLEMENTARY INFORMATION

Road Atlas to North America A number of road atlases are available from bookstores and gas stations. A particularly good one is put out by Quaker State and published by Gousha/Chek-Chart, P.O. Box 6227, San Jose, CA 95150. These atlases do little that good individual state maps do not do, but they make visiting several states a bit more convenient.

FREE Campgrounds U.S.A. edited by Mary VanMeer, 1983, published by The East Woods Press, Fast & McMillan Publishers, Inc., 429 East Boulevard, Charlotte, NC 28203, $9.95. This book lists an incredible number of free campgrounds and can make travelling from one climbing area to another much less expensive. Also, sometimes free alternatives can be found to the more convenient campgrounds listed in *The Climber's Guide to North America.*

How to Get to the Wilderness Without a Car by Lee W. Cooper, 1982, published by Lee Cooper Publisher, P.O. Box 4073, Malibu, CA 90265, $7.95. This book describes in detail public transportation to many of the wild areas that have climbing. In appendices, it also lists many of the trail hiking guides to the regions covered. For those without a car and not wanting to hitch-hike, this book may prove helpful.

Let's Go: USA annual, published by St. Martin's Press, 175 Fifth Avenue New York, NY 10010, $8.95. This is only one of many books on travelling in the US that could prove valuable to climbers with interests beyond the rocks. These books usually focus on cities and major recreation areas (e.g. National Parks) and cover historical overviews, interesting sights, hotels, restaurants, transportation. *Let's Go: USA* is written by the Harvard Student's Agencies, and focuses on budget travel for students. By listing Youth Hostels, campgrounds, and budget hotels, it is probably more interesting to climbers than most of the other books available. For the West Coast, there is also a *Let's Go: California and the Pacific Northwest* which is even more detailed.

American Youth Hostel Handbook 1332 I St. NW, Washington D.C. 20005, free with membership. Youth hostels are rarely available next to climbing areas, but they can often be relatively cheap and interesting places to stay while travelling or visiting cities (where camping is often not worth the hastle).

Climbing Magazine PO Box E, Aspen, CO 81611. Each issue lists climbing equipment stores that distribute the magazine. This can be a way of locating stores in cities between those listed in the *Climber's Guide to North America*.

50 Classic Climbs of North America by Steve Roper and Allen Steck, 1979, published by Sierra Club Books, 530 Bush Street, San Francisco, CA 94108, $10.95. Most of the climbs in this book are also found in the *Climber's Guide to North America*, but since *50 Classic Climbs* concentrate on individual routes, much more historical detail can be learned from it on these particular climbs.

Advanced Rockcraft by Royal Robbins, 1971, La Siesta Press, Box 406, Glendale, CA 91209, $3.95. Though not recent enough for the latest technology, this book gives an excellent introduction to big wall techniques.

Climb! Rock Climbing in Colorado by Bob Godfrey and Dudley Chelton, 1977, published by Alpine House, 873 8th Street, Boulder, CO 80302. This is an excellent and enjoyable treatment of the history of Colorado rock climbing, though it is recently out of print.

Vertigo Games by Glenn Randall, 1984. Published by W.R. Publications, 223 Cloverleaf Court, Sioux City, IA 51103. This soft cover, $20 book illustrates many modern Colorado free climbs with color photographs.

Beyond the Vertical by Layton Kor, 1984; published by Alpine House, 873 8th Street, Boulder, CO 80302. This hardcover book is historically exciting, has many superb color photographs, and costs $35.

ROCKY MOUNTAIN ROCK CLIMBS

Driving west from the Mississippi River, one travels a thousand miles through cornfields and prairies. Finally, a thin line can be seen on the horizon. As we continue on, the line gradually grows into a row of mountains that extend north-south as far the eye can see. But the road continues flat as a pancake to Boulder, Colorado—at the very foot of the Rocky Mountain foothills, and at the hub of Western climbing activities.

Boulder may not draw as many visiting climbers as California's fabled 'Climbing Mecca"—Yosemite Valley—but a good number of those who do visit Boulder eventually establish residence there. It is unlikely that any other large town (Boulder's 1985 population was about 70,000) has such a high percentage of climbers. And there is a good reason for this: probably no city in North America is surrounded by so much rock of such diversity, and of so high a quality.

Within a three minute drive from downtown, the granite outcroppings of Boulder Canyon become available. Within five minutes, Flagstaff presents world-renowned bouldering. Within ten minutes, the wonders of one of the world's finest climbing areas—Eldorado Canyon—are available. From here, and from the city itself, one can hike to the Flatirons—where frequently ignored climbing would alone put Boulder on the climber's map.

One hour from Boulder are the many splendors of Rocky Mountain National Park. It is two hours to Vedauwoo, the Garden of the Gods and the South Platte. Five hours presents the Canyonlands and Fremont, eight hours the Black Canyon, Devils Tower and the Needles. Only a few more miles yields a number of areas generally outside the sphere of influence of Boulder area climbers: Zion, the Sandias, Granite Mountain, Little Cottonwood Canyon, the City of Rocks, Blodgett Canyon—not to mention uncounted less known areas that are not included in this book.

To further spice the opportunities, Boulder's climate can permit rock climbing the year round—if not at the city limits, then within a few hour's drive. It is little wonder, then, that Boulder has so great a population of climbers from Europe, the Midwest and the East Coast.

The climbing in Boulder is diverse and is a microcosm of the diversity found throughout the Rocky Mountains. Though granite predominates, even this medium offers everything from the huge crystals of the sharply pointed Needles, to the smooth columns of the Devils Tower and the flared cracks of Lumpy Ridge. In size, the granite varies from one pitch routes in Vedauwoo to thirty pitch epics in the Black Canyon. The views vary from the narrow enclosure of Fremont Canyon to the expansiveness of the Diamond near the top of 14,255 foot Long's Peak; the climate covers the gamut from the northern winters of Montana's Blodget Canyon to the southern sunshine of Arizona's Granite Mountain.

All this has been simply a sampling of the *granite* areas. The other major rock type, sandstone, is almost as diverse, ranging from the loose flakes of the Garden of the Gods to the impeccable cracks of the Canyonlands. Sandstone routes vary from leisurely two hour climbs in the Flatirons to strenuous two day ascents in the spectacular canyon of Zion.

Geographically, the region is complex—as one would expect from such a large expanse of mountainous terrain. The Rocky Mountains themselves (including numerous sub-ranges that extend westward) stretch from near the Mexican border to near the Alaskan border. From the giant thrust fault that forms the start of the Front Range foothills (where they jut out of the vast Great Plains), one range after another extends westward for 500 miles to Nevada's Great Basin.

Subdividing the Rocky Mountains, we find the multiple ranges of Western Colorado to be the most extensive and the highest in elevation. Though few Colorado peaks even approach the vertical relief of the Alps or the Canadian Rockies, their average height is great enough to place Colorado at the top of the continental United States—with fifty three peaks in excess of 14,000 feet.

In generalized terms, Colorado's mountains can be thought of as extending from the Sandia Mountains in northern New Mexico to the eroding hills around Fremont Canyon in southern Wyoming. Some volcanic and sedimentary peaks exist in this expanse, but virtually all of the popular rock climbing areas are granite outcroppings. Never does one find exactly the smooth, glacially polished and incredibly clean granite that dominates California; instead, Rocky Mountain rock tends to be coarser, with a rough surface and more raggedly cracked faces. At the smoother end of the spectrum, Pike's Peak, Turkey Rocks, Lumpy Ridge and Vedauwoo offer continuous one to three pitch cracks. Aspen's rough-cut little crags, the Sandias' 500 foot cliffs with discontinuous crack systems, and the broken face of Telluride's Ophir Wall, all epitomize the ragged nature of the other end of the spectrum.

The granite that comprises the peaks of Rocky Mountain National Park is complex, varying from smoothly polished (as close as we come to Yosemite-like) to roughly chiseled.

The granite of the Black Canyon of the Gunnison is as variable as that in Rocky Mountain National Park, but its quality is often lower. This serious area may never be destined for mass popularity, but the intense climbing on its airy 2,000 foot walls has its attractions.

On the face of the Front Range, sedimentary beds were tilted upwards as the granite mountains pushed their way through. Here, at the very edge of the plains, the soft, flaky sandstone of the Garden of the Gods contrasts markedly with the solidly metamorphosed sandstone of Eldorado Canyon.

Northwest of Colorado, the Rocky Mountains take a respite in the plains of central Wyoming, then go into contorted spasms again as one approaches Montana. Wyoming's superb Teton and Wind River Ranges offer tremendous rock outcroppings that require approaches beyond the scope of this book. Western Montana is a vast expanse of forest-carpeted and mountain-ruptured wilderness. Projecting from a great number of mountains, hills, and valleys are granite cliffs that few climbers have ever heard of, let alone experienced. Blodgett Canyon is just a sample of what is available.

Directly west from Colorado's mountains and beyond the relatively flat expanse of the Colorado Plateau sits the last bastion of mountains before the vast desolation of the Great Basin: the Wasatch Range. Famous for its incredible powder skiing, the Wasatch also holds several fine rock outcroppings, including Little Cottonwood Canyon, near Salt Lake City. A hundred miles northwest of Salt Lake is Idaho's City of Rocks, an odd collection of hundred foot granite outcroppings near a small cluster of hills.

In the desert at the southern edge of the Colorado Plateau, we find countless sandstone canyons. Here (in the state of Utah) is the tremendous maze of Canyonlands National Park. The rock is cleaved by some of the most impecable cracks anywhere—not even the edges of the cracks are round; instead, everything is cut at sharp angles. The desert experience is as intense as the climbing experience, and it is a land for wonder and aesthetic appreciation, not a place simply for battle with rock.

Likewise Zion Canyon, at Utah's southwestern border, has sandstone walls that are inspiring just to see and touch. Where the Canyonlands holds 200-300 foot walls and sundry spires and towers, Zion displays 1,000 foot walls in a narrow canyon, with oddly shaped sandstone summits above.

Not fitting any geographical pattern, Devils Tower and the Needles are almost next to each other where northeastern Wyoming borders South Dakota. The Tower is a granitic plug, once the core of a volcano that has completely eroded away. Its columnar structure provides a tremendous number of cracks to climb. In the nearby Black Hills of South Dakota—an anomaly in a state renowned for its lack of topography—a conglomeration of fantastic granite pinnacles comprise the Needles. Though granite, these pinnacles are also an anomaly, as their giant pegmatite crystals are individually big enough for hand and footholds.

Also geographically lonely, at least in terms of areas covered in *The Climber's Guide to North America*, is central Arizona's Granite Mountain. Its single 500 foot face has a number of steep cracks on sound rock.

The weather for the Rocky Mountain region is almost as diverse as the areas to climb in. Still, the predominent pattern is sunny skies, with continental weather patterns. Except for Western Montana, the entire region is moderately to extremely arid. The precipitation that does fall is more likely to come in the form of winter snow and summer afternoon thundershowers than in extended periods of rain. Winters tend to be cold, and summers are usually hot, though the altitude of many areas is sufficient to moderate summer temperatures. The extremely low humidity also serves to keep temperatures more bearable. In fact, far more pleasurable mid-summer rock climbing can be found here than anywhere else in North America. The sun-filled skies can provide frequent midwinter climbing opportunities.

Geology and weather are not the only influences in the Rocky Mountain area climbing experience; demographics play at least as important a role. The region supports the greatest diversity of major rock climbing areas on the Continent and it is by far the least densely populated segment of the United States; it also nurtures some of the most protective and secretive groups of climbers in the world. This protectiveness is not just displayed by climbing area locals—indeed sometimes there are no locals—but also by metropolitan climbers who want to avoid seeing their favorite vacation haunts overrun by the climbing world at large.

Along the Colorado Front Range, from Colorado Springs in the south to Fort Collins in the north, one finds a barely broken chain of urban centers. This population will soon reach three million and is roughly

quivalent to the combined total of all three of the bordering Rocky
Mountain states. For the climber, this boils down to the obvious: Front
Range climbing will be more crowded than that found elsewhere in the
region.

Still, queues for climbs are rare, except on the most popular routes
n the most popular days. Though the large population might be the
downfall for wilderness in the Front Range, a great diversity of crags is
the salvation of its climbing. Those who want escape from crowds can
always find it. When concern is raised about overpopulating a remote
area, it generally comes down to not wanting to even see another climber
on a cliff, or not wanting one's favorite campsite to be taken; it isn't a
worry that the parking lot will spill over.

This is not to say that the Rockies are the Wild West, where man can
romple roughshod over the environment. Many of the West's most
beautiful areas have shown signs of abuse—by climbers and by other
recreational enthusiasts. The desert, in particular, is a fragile place, as
are alpine meadows and some subalpine scree slopes. To protect the
feeling of remoteness and wilderness beauty that so many of us crave
when we visit the Rocky Mountains' less populous areas, it is critically
important to step lightly, with a heightened awareness of our effects on
the environment and on fellow visiting climbers. If there are only two
climbing parties in the solitude of a remote area, try to make your own
climb on the next cliff down from the first people. Talk softly, and
remember that this is not a climber's gymnasium like Eldorado Canyon;
t must be treated differently. Only with appropriate respect will these
remote areas maintain their special character. Remember, that character
s why we have gone there in the first place.

A BRIEF HISTORY OF ROCK CLIMBING
IN THE ROCKY MOUNTAIN REGION

Early Rocky Mountain explorers climbed peaks to chart unexplored territory. Still, they were adventurers, for whom the thrill of being the first to a summit often had appeal beyond simple map-making. In 1806, Lt. Zebulon Pike made an attempt at hiking up what came to be known as Pike's Peak, and fourteen years later Edwin James led the ascent of this, the first 14,000 foot mountain to be climbed in North America.

Similar ascents took place by adventurous explorers with scientific pretences, including the 1868 first Caucasian ascent of Long's Peak, which has since become the most sought after climbing peak in the Rocky Mountains. (It is likely that Arapaho Indians made previous ascents to trap eagles on the summit.) Long's Peak, because of its height and prominence from Front Range population centers, became one of the first true recreational climbing mountains in the country. By 1890, when the first guidebook came out to the peaks of what would become Rocky Mountain National Park, hundreds of people per year were already climbing Long's. The nation's first climbing guide service was instituted there by the turn of the century. The population of the Front Range was no longer just struggling settlers; leisure time, tourists and money had come to the area—providing the means for playtime, including climbing.

Technical climbing may have been unknown in North America—despite a strong development of the sport in Europe by then—but the spirit of going where no one had gone before, on a difficult mountain face, was strong in the Reverend Elkanah Lamb as he meditated on the summit of Long's Peak in 1871. He walked over to the never climbed and much feared East Face and descended it, almost sliding to his death on the lower snow slope now appropriately named **Lamb's Slide**. Curiously, newspapers and the climbing world focused more on the "first ascent" of the East Face by James Alexander in 1922. During the intervening years, the East Face was downclimbed once again, in 1906 by Enos Mills, the person perhaps most responsible for the establishment of Rocky Mountain National Park in 1915.

Even Alexander, who's route later received a difficulty grading of 5.5 did his climb without any knowledge of the technical aspects of rock climbing. The first route on Long's Peak that involved modern rope-handling techniques was the audacious 1927 ascent of **Stettner's Ledges**. Joe and Paul Stettner were brothers from Munich who had learned to climb in their home Kaisergebirge before they moved to Chicago. They owned pitons, ice axes and carabiners, and knew how to use them on difficult rock. Though they did their route free at a 5.7 to 5.8 standard subsequent more "modern" ascents have often used aid. The Stettners came and went on their vacation climbs in Colorado with little or no fanfare and their routes played little role in directly stimulating local ctivity.

Albert Ellingwood left his home of Colorado Springs for college studies at Oxford, England, in 1910. In 1914 he brought home a knowledge of European style rope-handling and proceeded to make the most difficult ascents in Colorado—and possibly in the United States. He first established several 5.6 routes in the Garden of the Gods, then in 1920 teamed with Barton Hoag to climb the Lizard Head, a 350 foot volcanic plug whose summit lies at 13,113 feet in the San Juan Mountains of southern Colorado. This route is at least 5.7 in technical difficulty (Ellingwood may have used a point of aid) and is on loose rock in a remote setting. It was a landmark climb.

Lizard Head is also perhaps the most difficult summit to reach in Colorado. The fact that virtually every Colorado peak can be ascended by at most 3rd class scrambling probably had much to do with the lack of early technical development there. That there are over fifty 14,000 foot peaks to scramble up may have played a role in Colorado's lack of early influence on national developments in climbing.

Ellingwood's early ascents did little to spur mountaineers onto more difficult ground. This was but the first example of the lack of communication between Colorado Springs based climbers and those in the Denver-Boulder area. In Boulder, the self-proclaimed "thrill-seekers," who climbed on the east faces of the Flatirons, considered ropes cheating—but then, they had no concept of belaying either. To them, a rope was something for the first person up to drag behind so that less experienced climbers could grasp it as a hand-hold when needed. These thrill-seeking scramblers were active on the Flatirons for decades after the first ascent of the **East Face of the 3rd Flatiron** in 1906 by Floyd and Earl Millard. A thrill it must have been, for a fall on the face could be 1,300 feet long.

While Boulder area climbers were content to repeat their established routes and to only occasionally venture onto new ground, a group calling themselves the "San Juan Mountaineers" climbed many new routes during the 1920's and 30's, even publishing a pamphlet: *San Juan Mountaineer's Guide to Southwestern Colorado.* One of their leaders, Dwight G. Lavender, made the prophetic statement that it was more fun to practice on crags with a rope than it was to plod up 14,000 foot peaks. This view was hardly shared by the newly formed Colorado Mountain Club.

Still, neither Lavender's group nor the "thrill-seekers" pushed the standards of technical difficulty. During the 1930's Fritz Weissner passed through the Rockies, making the first climbing ascent of the Devils Tower (climbed originally by ranchers in 1893 who hammered a wooden ladder into a crack), and some serious technical mountaineering was being done in the Tetons (from which Wiessner was returning when he visited the Tower). But where contemporary rock climbers in California were willing to travel for hours to reach Yosemite and other crags, residents of the Front Range cities in Colorado, sometimes just minutes from the nearest rock, did little or nothing to truly test themselves. Indeed, Coloradans had little knowledge that anyone else in the country even practiced the sport.

A few exceptions to those willing to push themselves did exist. Most notable among them was Robert Ormes, who attempted Shiprock, a tremendous volcanic plug that rises almost 1,700 feet out of the New Mexican desert floor. Shiprock is certainly one of the most impressive rock "mountains" in North America, and was considered possibly the premier prize of its day. (It is not included in this book because it is located on Navajo reservation land; the Indians do not allow climbing on the reservation and their wishes should be respected.) Finally, Ormes took a twenty foot fall, terminating his attempts. The prize of Shiprock's summit was finally plucked in 1939 by the superior skills of a group of California climbers trained in Yosemite.

A few years after the war, rock climbing in Colorado began to re-emerge from the doldrums. Coloradans active in exploration were unaware of the rope handling techniques that were developed during the war and being advanced elsewhere. Brad Van Diver and Bill Eubank made first ascents of future classics like the **East Ridge of the Matron** and pioneered the incredible **Maiden Overhang** rappel. It took climbers of the late 1940's, led by Tom Hornbein, considerable time and effort to invent for themselves such basic tricks as using a sling for a foot-loop on aid moves. Aid climbing was further reinvented by Dale Johnson who would test nailing and belaying techniques on overhangs near the ground. These aid climbers were delighted when Roy Holubar began having pitons made locally to supplement the European soft-steel blade and the omnipresent (after the war) Army ring-angle pitons. The nvention of the first aluminum carabiners helped lighten the load of so much iron.

These climbers, oddballs in Colorado's world of "mountaineers"—i.e. mountain hikers—were audacious enough to soon want to put their kills to test on the major walls of the East Face of Long's Peak. Even he **Diamond** itself came under intense scrutiny. Tom Hornbein was a eader in probes onto the East Face, but in 1952, after traversing out into Table Ledge during a reconnaissance, he became convinced that he **Diamond** was out of the scope of his skills. Dale Johnson did not hare these feelings, and began laying plans for an attempt. He never ctually set foot on the cliff, however, for he made the mistake of asking he Park Service for permission; it was promptly denied. Further requests hrough the rest of the decade produced the same dogmatic refusal.

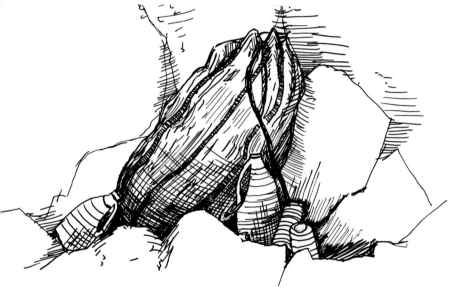

The Park Service's motives may have been misguided, but Johnson's elief that he was up for the challenge of the **Diamond** was probably aive. During the mid 1950's Colorado climbing was so far behind that racticed elsewhere in the country, California in particular, that the first scents of the Redgarden Wall in Eldorado and of the North Face of Iallett Peak, did not occur until 1956. Each of these climbs is only grade II 5.7, but each was a psychological breakthrough because of length 500-1,000 feet) and steepness. **The Redguard Route** was significant in 1at it opened the vast potential of Eldorado Canyon; Hallett was 1portant in breaking into the unknowns of a major "north face." Iallett's climb, by Ray Northcutt and Harvey T. Carter, briefly took on ninence from Carter's write-ups of the route as one of the nation's reat test pieces—this notion was promptly debunked in 1959 with a peedy second ascent by Yvon Chouinard and Ken Weeks.

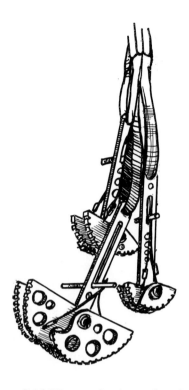

Another major event of 1956 was the introduction of Layton Kor into the climbing world. A quick glance at the first ascent record in almost any of Colorado's climbing areas quickly shows the influence of this incredibly energetic climber. He single handedly dominated the rock climbing scene from the late 1950's to the mid-1960's; all of the other prominent climbers played secondary roles in the region's rock climbing until Kor left the climbing scene in 1967. Fittingly, Ray Northcutt's premier and culminating climb, the **Diagonal** on the Lower East Face of Long's Peak made in 1959, was also Kor's first major route. But that year Northcutt made another contribution; goaded on by the untruth that Kor had free climbed a direct start to the **Bastille Crack**, Northcutt determined that he could do the route as well. He put up the Northcutt variation—thus making the first 5.10 ascent in the nation (some say it is actually 5.11).

To Kor, however, free climbing was of relatively little importance. He was exceedingly capable of free climbing, doing 5.9's and even occasional 5.10's in the early sixties, but placed little value in it. To him and to those he influenced—most of the leaders in the Colorado climbing population—speed was primary. The climbers were steeped in the legends of Europe, where they read of the necessity for speed on big mountains. To step on a piton was trivial—far better than to waste time iguring out the moves free. Because of the quantity of virgin rock that climbers of the 1950's had at their disposal, competitive conflicts over the style of an ascent were rare. During the late 1950's Kor, with a series of partners—most notably Bob Culp—established Eldorado Canyon as the primary focus for hard-core rock climbers.

Kor's attitude on style reflected that of the majority of the Rocky Mountain climbing population—that is, climbers based in the Boulder region. In Colorado Springs, climbers took a slightly different approach. Influenced originally by Ellingwood's British attitude concerning the minimal use of pitons, they continued this tradition. Harvey T. Carter began climbing there in the 1950's and soon became one of the region's more influential climbers. He developed a technique to reduce the damage that pitons caused in the incredibly soft sandstone at the Garden of the Gods. His technique involved drilling holes in the rock, into which Army ring-angle pitons were driven and left fixed. This not only saved the cracks, but it opened the potential of the Garden's great faces that are sometimes devoid of cracks. In keeping with Ellingwood's tradition of minimal piton use, Carter would deliberately place his protection in positions where they could offer no aid on crux moves, and he would space them widely. Harvey T. Carter was influential outside of the small Colorado Springs climbing community in that he was one of the first Coloradans to travel to other climbing centers around the country.

In 1960 two Californians passed through Colorado and took with them the state's most sought after first ascent: **the Diamond**. The Park Service had decided to open the cliff to climbing and had sent applications to a number of interested parties. Kor was touring Europe and North America that summer, and the few other Coloradans who were capable of the ascent did not act quickly enough; Bob Kamps and Dave Rearick swooped in and scooped up the prize. In the tradition of Park Service bureaucracy, they required (and continued to require for several years) that Diamond climbers assemble both primary and secondary support parties.

If Colorado climbers felt that they had been robbed of their gemstone, they were also beginning to feel the pressure of being left behind in the free-climbing standards that were rising elsewhere in the country. Kor travelled widely in the early 1960's and expressed his energies at home as well, but he was always more interested in getting up new routes than in freeing them. A Californian, Royal Robbins, was perhaps most instrumental in pointing Coloradans towards the competitive esthetics of free climbing. His visit in 1963 produced a lightning-fast one day ascent of a new route on the **Diamond** with Kor, but his 1964 visit stunned the locals with his free climbing skills and attitudes. Not only did he try to free everything he attempted, but he was willing to take short falls during those attempts. **Athlete's Feat** (5.10+) on Castle Rock was perhaps his finest achievement. Young Pat Ament partnered Robbins on many of his climbs and continued in Robbin's absence as a leader in Colorado free climbing. Ament was a prime mover in firmly establishing the 5.10 standard in Colorado and then helped with the 5.11 standard when its turn came. Larry Dalke, originally one of the region's best aid climbers, and Dave Rearick, who had moved to Colorado following his ascent of the **Diamond**, were others who helped establish 5.10.

Robbins also visited Little Cottonwood Canyon in 1964. There he teamed up with Ted Wilson, one of two or three locals who had reached the 5.9 standard, to climb the Canyon's first 5.10. The Salt Lake region did not long need outside spurs, however, as Mark McQuarrie and George Lowe, followed soon by George's cousins Jeff and Greg Lowe, began climbing desperate 5.10 leads. In 1965, McQuarrie and George climbed the **Dorsal Fin**. With four hard pitches—5.10+, 5.10, 5.9, 5.8— this may have been the most difficult, or at least the most continuously difficult, climb in the country. McQuarrie, one of the nation's most inspired and talented climbers, died when his rope severed over an edge; George and Jeff have gone on to become preeminent figures in the alpine and Himalayan climbing scenes.

While the free climbing revolution was beginning in the Rockies, Kor continued a frenetic pace of exploration, searching out sandstone spires in the southwestern desert and pioneering grade V routes in the Black Canyon. He led virtually every team that climbed in the Black until his final attempts at a route on the **Painted Wall** in 1967. 1967 also saw Kor, with Wayne Goss, make the first winter ascent of the **Diamond**. Then he dropped out of the climbing world entirely, redirecting his energies to religion and building a family.

With him passed an era, because as the 1970's approached, so did an emphasis on short, hard free routes; aid was virtually eliminated from the repertoire of Boulder's crag climbers. A consciousness of the environmental degradation of piton usage helped the move to nuts and free climbing, but most important was the competition to improve style when so little room was left available for entirely new routes. Further facilitating the move to free climbing was an increase in national interchange (not just through increased travel, but also through the founding of national magazines like *Climbing*).

Jim Erickson emerged during this period as a principal leader in establishing style as an idealogical basis for climbing, and remarkably he simultaneously consolidated the 5.10 standard and launched into 5.11. After freeing the **Naked Edge** in Eldorado with Duncan Ferguson (including three pitches of 5.11, in 1971), he concluded that to fall was to "taint" the route by providing the climber with prior knowledge of the moves before actually succeeding. His goal became to climb only in such a way that he could have succeeded had there been no rope for safety.

Erickson's high sense of style most certainly did not become *de rigeu* for the rest of the climbing community, but it was important in helping to establish that it was not what, but *how* one climbed that counted during this period. When Jim Logan and Wayne Goss made the long awaited (and often attempted) first free ascent of the **Diamond** in 1975, they carried only nuts for protection and brought no emergency gear; they treated this most intimidating of faces as if it were a Sunday outing on the local crag. Style mattered here, just as it did closer to the ground. Another leader of this period was Steve Wunsch, who freed an incredible number of routes, including the poorly protected **Jules Verne** (5.11), in Eldorado.

Aid climbing was was still necessary for most routes in the Black Canyon. Bill Forrest and Kris Walker made the first ascent of the hideously loose **Painted Wall**. That same summer, a team from Arizona also ascended the Painted Wall, but via a different route. The first climb involved eight days of climbing, the second nine days. Colorado's first, and only, Grade VI's were born.

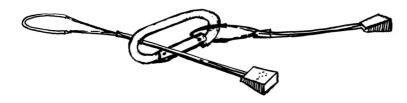

As free climbing became the norm in the 1970's, so did the interchange of climbers from around the country. Still, Colorado Springs climbers and Boulder climbers only infrequently mixed. When Springs climbers needed diversity from their crumbling Garden of the Gods dinner plate holds and from the local (and very secretly held) granite cliffs of Pike's Peak and the South Platte (including Turkey Rocks), they would venture to the desert of the Canyonlands and to the Black Canyon.

In the Black Canyon in particular, they established climbs with extraordinary difficulty and commitment. Jim Dunn and Earl Wiggins put up a number of routes that have rarely if ever been repeated—both free and aid climbs. They free climbed Kor's infamous **Diagonal**—a Grade V route on which Kor had spent eight hours nailing a single pitch which he declared to be the most difficult and dangerous pitch of his prolific career. Their motto for this and other climbs was: a rope and a rack, and the shirts on our backs. Wiggins free-soloed the **Scenic Cruise** via a new variation in 90 minutes (grade V 5.10 +), and Jim Dunn took Black Canyon skills to Yosemite, to make the first solo first ascent on El Capitan. Springs climber Leonard Coyne in 1981 teamed with Californian Randy Leavitt to free climb the **Painted Wall**, producing 30 dangerous pitches with sections of 5.11 + protected by widely spaced copperheads. After a couple of attempts, they climbed it in a day. Peripatetic Ed Webster emerged from Colorado Springs as well.

The 1970's saw numerous crags away from the major climbing population centers come into heavy use. Ever since Herb and Jan Conn moved into the Needles in the late 1940's, they had attempted to lure fellow climbers to visit South Dakota. In the 1950's and 60's, a small group of climbers from various areas around the country, most notably California, would gather for the summer in the cool beauty of the Black Hills. The 1970's finally saw more climbers visit the Needles, though most were just passing through on their way to Devils Tower—by then a major magnet for climbers as well as other tourists. Telluride's Ophir Wall came into slightly greater prominence as Royal Robbins' Mountaincraft climbing school taught there for several years. The Sandias in New Mexico and the many crags of Montana, including Blodgett Canyon, also saw increased traffic during this period, though mostly from locals. Indeed, if climbers emerged during the fifties and sixties principally from population centers, during the seventies many developed near small or less-known areas. Zion, for example, was originally climbed almost entirely by visitors from Salt Lake City and Colorado before residents (including some who had moved there) took up the sport.

The end of the 1970's saw the establishment of 5.12 throughout the region, including what may still be the region's face climbing testpiece: **Genesis** in Eldorado, by Jim Collins. This climb, and one of Colorado's earliest 5.13's—**Sphinx Crack** in the South Platte—required many days of sieging before their eventual success.

Perhaps the most significant rock climbing event in the Rocky Mountains, one that continues unabated into the eighties, is the influx of climbers into Boulder. Nationwide, the actual numbers of participants in the sport may have stopped growing. But those who already climb have visited Eldorado among their wide-ranging travels—and many of them have decided that the Colorado Front Range is a rock climber's version of heaven on earth. They have since made Boulder their home— perhaps the best way to get around the lack of adequate camping in the area.

Chris Jones' book, *Climbing in North America*, offers the only comprehensive history of climbing on the continent. Because this fascinating book presents history by tracing the flow of events instead of simply reciting the facts, it provides very entertaining reading, at home or by fire-light. Everyone interested in the historical development of climbing on this continent is urged to read the book. Published in 1976 for the American Alpine Club by the University of California Press, Berkeley, CA. Available from the American Alpine Club, 113 East 90th Street, New York NY 10028, hardback $19.95, paperback $9.95, plus $1.25 postage.

Several other recommended books will be found in the bibliography. These books, the climbing magazines and the guidebooks listed in each chapter form the source material for this essay.

John Harlin on Wine and Roses photo: Arno Ilgner

Granite Mountain photo: Dan Hare

The landscape photo: Gregg Lindsay

GRANITE
MOUNTAIN

HIGHLIGHTS

While Arizona is world famous as the "Grand Canyon State," holding one of the earth's great natural wonders, among rock climbers it remains in undeserved obscurity. This anonymity is a boom to local privacy seekers because the state's plethora of superb granite is a delight for visiting climbers. A guidebook, occasional magazine articles, and considerable word of mouth reporting have made Granite Mountain the best known of the many obscure areas scattered throughout the state. Its granite is solid if sometimes a bit coarse. The semi-arid environment is hilly, vegetated with high desert scrub and features plenty of sunshine; it often permits year-round climbing. Convenient camping and good bouldering are available nearby.

CLIMBING

Granite Mountain is a large outcropping of rock set high on a hillside. Its single face, 1,000 yards in breadth, displays different characters of climbing on its different facets. The western end, the "Swamp Slabs," is low-angle and holds a number of high quality beginner and moderate routes. Moving right, the cliff becomes steeper, though cleaved by large chimneys and cracks, and features harder routes. The dominant aspect of the crag is its vertical 500 foot high central section, which sports mostly difficult routes, often of an unrelenting nature. To the right of the Flying Buttress, a large, exceptionally compact and little blemished piece of rock, one reaches a diverse series of two pitch faces that provides thin slab and steep crack climbing.

The rock on Granite Mountain has some of the rough and flakey characteristics typical of arid-region, non-glaciated granite, but it is generally very solid and trustworthy.

Route gradings at Granite Mountain are notoriously stiff. These stiff ratings result partially from their development in an out-of-the-main-stream climbing area. The lack of traffic in general, and the infrequent ascents of those few routes that require pitons (usually aid routes), results in exceptionally pristine cracks and a general sense that climbers have done little to alter the rock or the environment. This is further evidenced by a reluctence among many locals to use chalk.

ENVIRONMENT

At an elevation of about 7,500 feet, Granite Mountain is high enough in the hills to avoid most of Arizona's infamous summer heat, but it is far enough south that winters are often mild—or at least have mild periods. However, the first guidebook to the crag credits local lore with a saying that in Arizona, only newcomers and fools predict the weather. Still, sunshine is the norm, as evidenced by the shrubs, adapted to semi-arid climates, and the paucity of substantial trees.

Nearby Prescott College is an exciting school that trains many outdoor educators and administrators; outdoors-oriented students found here are often enthusiastic and ready partners for climbing.

CLIMBING HISTORY
Granite Mountain is youthful in its climbing history— surprisingly so for being situated less than ten miles from a dynamic college town. The first recorded technical route was not established until 1966, followed by little significant activity until the early 1970's. During the 1970's, Prescott College students, an informal Southwestern climbing club, the Syndicato Granitica, and several well travelled and highly skilled visitors combined to climb most of the obvious lines on the crag, yielding about seventy-five routes and variations. Standards during this period were always high, and free attempts on the few aid routes came not long after their establishment. Unfortunately, this rapid pace meant that in a short time only a few outrageously difficult lines remained to be free climbed. Today, Granite Mountain offers little for locals to explore and develop, but it provides a rich lode of excellent routes for all to enjoy.

CAMPING
A National Forest campground, Granite Basin, provides convenient tenting for Granite Mountain climbers. Its fee of $4 includes water and tables, but other facilities must be found in nearby Prescott.

SEASONS AND WEATHER

Approximate Months	Typical Temperatures High	Low	Likelihood of Precipitation	Frequency of Climbable Days
Dec-Feb	40's −	10's	low-med	med-low
Mar-Jun	60's −	30's	low-med	very high
Jul-Aug	70's +	50's −	medium	high
Sep-Nov	60's	30's	low	very high

Comments: Weather patterns are extremely variable. Brief but violent afternoon thundershowers are common in the summer.

RESTRICTIONS AND WARNINGS
The southern exposure, dry air, and lack of nearby water combine to make dehydration a nuisance. Be sure to bring plenty of water. There are also many furry critters eager to make off with poorly stashed lunches. Spring water should probably be treated.

GUIDEBOOKS
A *Topo Guide to Granite Mountain* (1982) by Jim Waugh. Available at many western climbing stores or from Polar Designs, 4431 E. 26th Ave, Denver, CO 80207. This little book is well designed and ready for abuse; it is printed on waterproof, tear-resistant paper.

GUIDE SERVICES AND EQUIPMENT STORES
Climbing shops can be found in Flagstaff and Phoenix.

EMERGENCY SERVICES
In case of emergency, notify the Yavapai County Sheriff at 445-2231. The nearest hospital is in Prescott: Yavapai Community Hospital, 1003 Willow Creek Road, telephone 445-2700.

GETTING THERE
Greyhound buses serve Prescott from Flagstaff or Phoenix, where major airlines can be located.

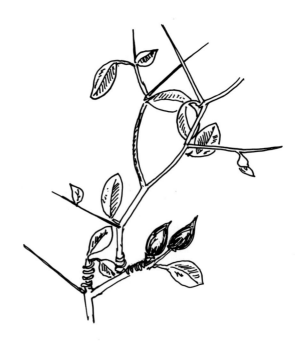

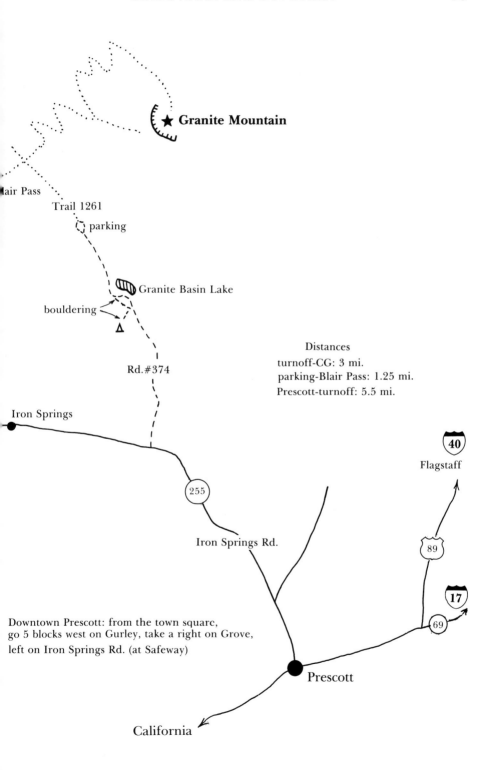

Granite Mountain

Blair Pass

Trail 1261

parking

Granite Basin Lake

bouldering

Rd.#374

Distances
turnoff-CG: 3 mi.
parking-Blair Pass: 1.25 mi.
Prescott-turnoff: 5.5 mi.

Iron Springs

40
Flagstaff

255

Iron Springs Rd.

89

17

69

Downtown Prescott: from the town square,
go 5 blocks west on Gurley, take a right on Grove,
left on Iron Springs Rd. (at Safeway)

Prescott

California

West Side photo: Gregg Lindsay
1 **Crawl 5.7** Rusty Baillie, David Lovejoy, Jonathan Bjorklund and Kent Madin, 1970.
2 **Debut 5.5** Rusty Baillie, David Lovejoy and Jack Hauck, 1970.
3 **Dislocation Direct 5.6** David Lovejoy, Jonathan Bjorklund and Kent Madin, 1971.
4 **Dislocation Buttress 5.4** Larry and Becky Treiber, 1969.

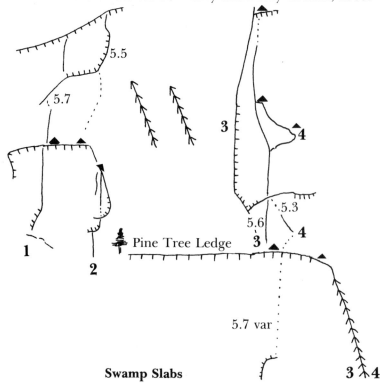

Chip Chace on Thin Slice direct finish

Middle Section photo: Dan Hare

Nose Rt.

16 var

17

Middle Section photo: Dan Hare

Large nuts (to 3"–3½") needed for most routes.

5 **Hassayampa 5.8 –** Karl Karlstrom and David Lovejoy, 1971.

6 **Magnolia Thunder Pussy 5.8 +** David Lovejoy, Jack Hauck and Jonathan Bjorklund, 1970. FFA: Karl Karlstrom, David Lovejoy and Scott Baxter, 1971.

7 **Green Savior 5.8** (or 5.9 direct start) Scott Baxter and Tom Taber, 1969.

8 **Gunsmoke Variation 5.12** John Long, Lynn Hill and Keith Cumming, 1980 (with preplaced protection). Large friends almost essential.

9 **Sorcerer 5.11** Marty Woener, David Lovejoy and Jack Hauck, 1971. FFA: Jim Waugh and John Ficker, 1981.

10 **Kingpin 5.10** Scott Baxter and Karl Karlstrom, 1972.

11 **Coatimundi Whiteout 5.11 –** Scott Baxter and Jim Whitfield, 1971. FFA 1st 2 pitches: Scott Baxter and Lee Dexter, 1971; FFA complete route: John Long, Lynn Hill and Keith Cumming, 1980. Friends especially helpful.

12 **Candyland 5.10 –** David Lovejoy and Dwight Bradley, 1970. FFA: Dan Hare and Scott Woodruff, 1973.

Coatimundi Whiteout-Candyland link-up 5.9

13 **Karl's Korner 5.9** Scott Baxter and Karl Karlstrom, 1968. FFA: Karl Karlstrom and Tom Taber, 1970.

14 **Classic 5.7** Scott Baxter, Karl Karlstrom and Lee Dexter, 1968.

15 **Reunion 5.10 –** Scott Baxter and Jim Whitefield, 1971. FFA: Scott Baxter and Karl Karlstrom, 1971.

16 **Said and Done 5.9** Jonathan Bjorklund and Bill Claggett, 1971. FFA: Rusty Baillie and Jack Hauck, 1971. *var.* **Help Me Mr. Wizard 5.11 +** Stan Mish, Jim Waugh and Herb North Jr., 1978.

17 **Cat's Pajamas 5.8 +** Jonathan Bjorklund, Bill Claggett and Bob Ladd, 1971. FFA: Larry Treiber and Chuck Parker, 1973.

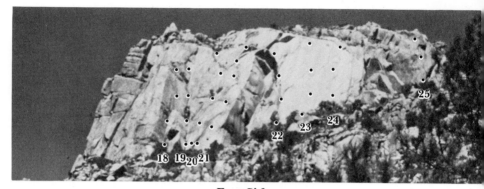

East Side photo: Chip Chase

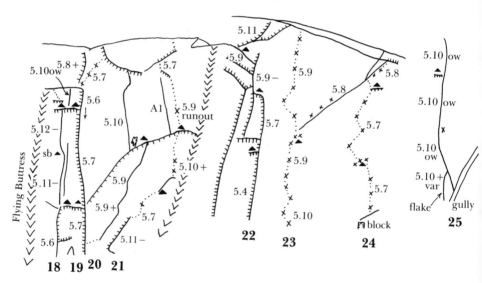

East Side

18 Twin Cracks 5.12 − Lance and Dane Daugherty, 1968. FFA: Jim Waugh and Dylan Williams, 1980. Bring many small nuts.

19 Coke Bottle 5.7 Don Weaver, Rex Lambert and John Brucker, 1967.

20 Falling Ross 5.10 Larry and Becky Treiber, 1969. FFA 2nd pitch: Scott Baxter and Karl Karlstrom, 1973; FFA complete route: David Anderson and Robert Crawford, 1974.

21 Adam's Rib 5.11 − Ed Webster and Larry Coates, 1977. FFA 3rd pitch: Jim Waugh and Jim Zahn, 1980.

22 Chieu Hoi 5.9 Scott Baxter and Karl Karlstrom, 1971.

23 Thin Slice 5.10 Marty Woerner and John Diaz, 1971. Direct finish: Soft Walk var. Larry Treiber, Scot Kronberg and Chuck Parker, 1973.

24 Bleak Streak 5.8 Scott Baxter, Karl Karlstrom and David Kolpin, 1971.

25 Jump Back Jack Crack 5.10 Karl Karlstrom, Scott Baxter and Rusty Baillie, 1972. Tube chocks helpful.

John Tiangco on Thin Slice photo: Chip Chace

Yataghan and Chaos Crag from the La Luz Trail

SANDIAS

HIGHLIGHTS

As a climbing area, Sandia Mountain is full of surprises. Though little known outside New Mexico, it overlooks the large city of Albuquerque; in the midst of the infamous Southwestern heat, it is cool and its best climbing season is midsummer; notorious for loose rock, its better routes are usually quite solid. Dozens of rough granite cliffs sprout from the upper reaches of massive Sandia Mountain. They average about 500 feet in height and are quite steep—frequently vertical. The routes follow discontinuous crack systems and involve a liberal mixture of crack and face climbing techniques. Sandias climbers must accept occasional run-outs and rock that can require special care to avoid knocking off loose blocks. Though camping is free, it involves staying either in a paved parking lot or hiking some distance into the nearby woods.

CLIMBING

Over the ages, a giant fault has lifted Sandia Mountain out of the surrounding flat desert of the Rio Grande Valley. The upper reaches of the mountain are adorned by steep cliffs that are sometimes simply cut out of the hillside, while in other instances erosion has given a cliff its own independent summit. The most massive cliff of the region, the 1,200 foot Shield, is difficult to reach and is frequently closed to climbing to protect nesting peregrine falcons; it has not been included in this book. Most of the cliffs that have been included—the Muralla Grande, Yataghan, El Torreon and the Thumb—average about 600 feet in height.

Because these cliffs have never seen the polishing touch of glaciers, the granite is coarse and generally offers an excellent grip. Fixed protection is rare on many of these routes and good route finding skills can be a necessity. Most climbs are infrequently travelled, reducing the likelihood of following a "white dotted" chalk line. The lack of traffic also means that loose blocks may not be cleaned up as thoroughly here as they would be at a more popular area. The most popular routes are relatively clean.

Many climbs are approached from above even though the cliffs won't be seen until the end of a half hour hike. With a little forethought and care, walking shoes and excess baggage can usually be left at the top of the cliff during the approach. This will prove quite welcome compared to the chore of returning to the base of the climb. (Be warned that finding the cliff from above can be tricky during the first search. Finding them from below is more dependable.)

The discontinuity of Sandias cracks systems requires a climber to be equally adept at face and crack climbing. In fact, even next to the cracks the rock may offer a plethora of excellent edges that can provide an alternative to jamming.

Just below the crest of Sandia Mountain—and above the granite cliffs—is a limestone band of remarkably high quality. Excellent top-roping problems can be found here.

ENVIRONMENT

From the flat, dry plains surrounding the urban sprawl of Albuquerque, one looks up 5,000 feet to the 10,600 foot Crest of Sandia Mountain. While sweltering in Albuquerque's 100 degree heat, it is hard to imagine that up on the Crest climbers might be shivering, anxiously awaiting an afternoon rain cloud to pass. Conversely, on a cold and windy night at the Crest, it is difficult to imagine that the houses making such a beautiful display of lights might actually have their air conditioners turned on. The contrast in climate and scenery between the Sandia Crest and the Rio Grande Valley below could not be greater, and for this reason many non-climbers hike, drive or take the tram to the Crest on weekends.

The nine-mile La Luz trail leaves from the Juan Tabo picnic area several miles from town. For the visiting climber, however, especially those planning to camp out, the drive to the Crest is a popular option. The road first encircles the mountain, then winds up the back-side before spitting one out on the very Crest itself. Here, a restaurant and souvenir store offer creature comforts after the climb.

Taking the tram is a spectacular, albeit expensive ($7.50) alternative to driving up. The 2.7 mile trip passes over many seldom visited crags. From the top of the tram, one must simply walk an extra mile (with expansive and airy views westward) to the main climbing areas.

CLIMBING HISTORY

The Needle is possibly the most "mountain-looking" of the granite crags scattered near Sandia's Crest, and as such it received the earliest attention of technically inclined climbers. In the 1940's this and a few other lower 5th class routes were ascended.

During the next two decades, disparate groups of climbers plied Sandia rock. Little communication existed between them, and often one group would rediscover, unknowingly, routes that had been ascended by previous groups.

Even if climbers of the 1960's opened a number of new lines, they were still a non-competitive group who showed little interest in the difficult routes being pioneered at leading climbing centers around the country. All of their routes stayed in the comfortable mid-5th class range, and indeed, it was not until the mid-1970's that even 5.9 was introduced to the Sandias. An article from the late 1960's states a preference to rate climbs with adjectives like 'Interesting,' 'Hairy,' 'Ecch,' instead of the Decimal System.

A new route boom occured from the mid-1970's into the 1980's, though even this "boom" continued in a relatively laid-back, non-competitive fashion. Climbers capable of top standard routes had begun developing these local crags, but their numbers were still small and the cliff supply is vast.

It may be surprising that such good rock, located so close to a major population center, would remain in the backwash of North American climbing. But such are the Sandias; and perhaps in that lies part of their charm.

CAMPING

Beautiful camping can be found with some exploratory hikes down the western side of the Crest. There are no designated sites and no campfire scars, so please leave this area in as natural a state as it was found. Less scenic, but more convenient to the car, would be to sleep in the parking lot. The lower lot offers peace and quiet from Friday and Saturday night teenage partying in the upper lot. Toilet facilities and a restaurant exist on the Crest, but no water is available.

SEASONS AND WEATHER

Approximate Months	Typical Temperatures High	Low	Likelihood of Precipitation	Frequency of Climbable Days
Nov-Mar	30's +	0's	med-high	low
Apr-May	50's −	20's −	medium	medium
Jun-Aug	70's	40's	med-high	high
Sep-Oct	60's −	30's +	medium	med-high

Comments: Most of the cliffs face westward, making them sometimes chilly in the morning. Despite its southern location, the weather follows Rocky Mountain patterns, including frequent afternoon rain showers and wind. July is usually the rainiest summer month. Small cliffs and boulders can be found in the warmer low elevations. From November until April or May, heavy snow cover can hinder access to the cliffs.

RESTRICTIONS AND WARNINGS

Because the Sandias are a falcon nesting area, local Forest Service authorities should be consulted for seasonal climbing restrictions, especially on the Shield. Cliff closures may vary each year, depending on the falcon's nesting whims. Descents from Torreon, Yataghan and the Thumb can be tricky and sufficient daylight will be needed to negotiate them. Loose rock and runouts must also be anticipated, as well as mountainous weather.

GUIDEBOOKS

Hikers and Climbers Guide to the Sandias (1983) by Mike Hill. Available from Albuquerque stores or by mail from the Wilderness Centre, 2421 San Pedro Drive NE, Albuquerque, NM 87110.

GUIDE SERVICES AND EQUIPMENT STORES

Though no guide services serve the Sandias, Albuquerque equipment shops include the Wilderness Centre, at 2421 San Pedro Dr NE; Sandia

Mountain Outfitters, at 1406 Eubank Blvd NE; Backwoods, at 6307 Menaul Boulevard NE; and Strings and Spokes, at 3222 Central Avenue SE.

EMERGENCY SERVICES

Mountain rescue organizations exist in the Albuquerque and Santa Fe area. They can be reached through the State Police at 841-8066 or 911 in an emergency. There is a phone inside the summit restaurant/gift shop. Albuquerque hospitals include: University of New Mexico Hospital, 2211 Lomas Boulevard NE, 843-2111 or emergency at 843-2411; and the Presbyterian Hospital, 1100 Central SE, 841-1234 or emergency room 841-1111.

GETTING THERE

All methods of public transportation serve Albuquerque, from which a car can be rented. Bus lines do not serve any access points, but a taxi could be used to reach either the trail or the tram.

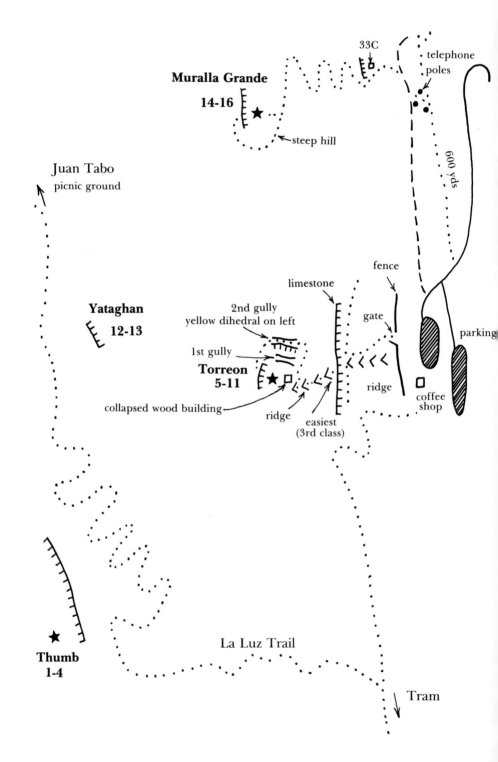

Muralla Grande
14-16

33C

telephone
poles

←steep hill

600 yds

Juan Tabo
picnic ground

fence

limestone

gate

Yataghan
12-13

2nd gully
yellow dihedral on left

parking

1st gully

Torreon
5-11

ridge

collapsed wood building

ridge

easiest
(3rd class)

coffee
shop

La Luz Trail

Thumb
1-4

Tram

Shield

Needle

Muralla Grande

Thumb

Yataghan

Torreon

The west face of Sandia Mountain

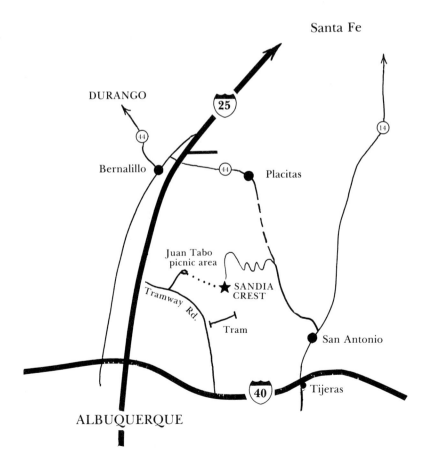

Santa Fe

DURANGO

25

14

Bernalillo

44

Placitas

14

Juan Tabo
picnic area

SANDIA
CREST

Tramway Rd.

Tram

San Antonio

40

Tijeras

ALBUQUERQUE

North Face of the Thumb

1 **North Summit Direct III 5.8** Reed Cundiff and David Hammack, 1960.
2 **Pumping Lichen III 5.11 −** Lee Sheftel and Peter Prandoni, 1983.
3 **Aviary Ort Overhangs III 5.9 +** Doug Bridgers and Rick Meleski, 1975.
4 **Northwest Ridge III 5.5** Stay left of ridge to start (on ridge harder). Great views!

North Face of the Thumb

Torreon and Mexican Breakfast

Mexican Breakfast Crack photo: Carl W. Smith

'orreon

5 Tarantula II 5.11 − Peter Prandoni and Jenny McKernan, 1976. Can be done in 1 pitch; less rope drag with 2.

6 Mexican Breakfast Crack II 5.9 − Doug Bridgers and Wayne Taylor, 1974. Crux is passing overhang. Above overhang, offwidth up crack or do easier face climbing to right.

Lee Sheftel on Wizard of Odd

Torreon

Descent: Scramble to summit, rappel to notch, and 3rd class up.

7 **Sorcerer's Apprentice III 5.11 –** Peter Prandoni, Gary Hicks and Doug Bridgers, 1979.

8 **Voodoo Child III 5.12 A0** First pitches Lee Sheftel and Peter Prandoni, completed by Peter Prandoni and Doug Bridgers, 1983. All the moves have been done free, but rests were taken on aid.

9 **Mountain Momma III 5.10** Dennis Udall and Dirk VanWinkle, 1977. The classic route on Torreon.

10 **Bitch's Brew III 5.11** Peter Prandoni and Ron Beauchamp, 1981.

11 **Wizard of Odd III 5.10 –** Mike Roybal, Peter Prandoni and Doug Bridgers, 1980.

Torreon

Yataghan

Yataghan – Upper Southeast Face photo: Carl W. Smith

Yataghan

12 The Happy Gnome III 5.8-5.10+ Rick Meleski and Doug Bridgers, 1974.
5.10 variation: Peter Prandoni and Greg McFarland, 1976. Keeping the
route at 5.8 may prove difficult; some runouts.

13 Southeast Face III 5.7 Reed Cundiff and David Hammack, 1960.

Liz Klobusicky-Mailander on Warpy Moople

Muralla Grande and the Crest

Muralla Grande
photo: David M. Benyak

**14 La Selva Route III
5.7** Rick Meleski and
Doug Bridgers, 1974.

**15 Warpy Moople III
5.10−** Mike Roybal and
Peter Prandoni, 1975.
The classic route on
Muralla Grande.

**16 The Second Coming III
5.8-5.10** depending on finish Joe Darriau and Thad
Meyerriecks, 1976.

East Temple

ZION NATIONAL PARK

HIGHLIGHTS

Among climbers, descriptions of Zion often involve comparisons with Yosemite's fabled Valley. The cliffs rise almost as magnificently above the canyon floor, a road with many tourists follows the river's course, and climbers can occasionally be spotted bivouacking high on a wall. But Zion's sandstone canyon is much narrower than Yosemite's open valley, and the rocks are far more colorful. Because the canyon sees few climbers, many of the excellent routes have rarely, if ever, been repeated. During the prime early spring and fall climbing seasons, neither the routes nor the campgrounds are congested. Zion's cliffs are a unique experience, providing climbers with an unforgettable visit.

CLIMBING

Despite over a decade of serious climbing, and some publicity, Zion continues to be be a relatively undeveloped area. Many visitors have preferred to climb new routes instead of repeating existing ones, and only a few routes have been ascended many times. This, combined with

the nature of sandstone climbing, means that Zion routes often have
more of an adventurous, unknown quality than routes in more popular
granite areas.

Zion's Navajo Sandstone yields superb crack climbing with peculiarities
unique to this type of rock. Most outstanding are the tremendous walls
rarely found in sandstone. Rising up to 2,000 feet in height, these cliffs
offer both free and aid climbing routes. Most climbs on major walls are
Grade V, while many shorter routes ascend smaller cliffs and cracks
along the base of the walls. Outside of the most popular and most
accessible canyon described in this book lie a number of excellent routes
often on walls just as large as the better known ones in the main canyon

The bottom half of the Navajo sandstone found in Zion is cemented
by iron oxides (which imparts the red coloration) and calcium carbonate
The red walls of the lower Navajo (800-1,200 feet) offer the best quality
climbing. Almost invariably, routes terminate at the so-called "false rim,"
above which lower angled white cliffs (also part of the Navajo) continue
upwards to the true canyon rim. These white cliffs offer some climbing
but the quality is usually dubious at best.

Even in the first thousand feet of red rock, the quality can vary
enormously. Although routes in this book are on the better rock
occasional loose sections will be encountered. It is important to test holds
carefully before using them and to be aware that large blocks and flakes
can be loose. An understanding of the rock can often be gained from
a single long ascent.

While most routes follow cracks, some superb face climbing can also
be found. Once the initial loose holds are removed, subsequent parties
may find such climbing safe and enjoyable.

The difficulty of fully trusting protection in soft sandstone can make
aid climbing a slower process than on quality granite. This extra time
needs to be taken into consideration when planning an ascent of a longer
route. Climbs tend to take much longer than they would appear to from
the ground.

Some important features of aid climbing and bolt protection on Zion
sandstone need to be noted. Often, instead of filling a drilled hole with
a bolt, as would be done in granite, the hole is left unfilled, into which
either a 3/8 inch copperhead (#3) is placed and removed by hand, or a
half inch angle piton is driven and removed by hammer blows. Use
copperheads whenever possible on the lead.

With belay anchors, the holes are intended for pitons, and often the
only reason they have not been left fixed is economic; subsequent ascent
parties are encouraged to bring extra half inch pins and to leave a few
fixed. Some climbers choose to use glued bolts instead of pitons. When
holes are encountered while aid climbing, they will frequently be much
too shallow for half inch pins; these are normally intended for insertion
of 3/8 inch copperheads and are not meant to be permanently filled. The
copperhead serves the same function as a bat-hook in granite— however

bat hooks SHOULD NOT be used in Zion's drilled holes as they will rapidly destroy the rock. On longer "bolted" blank sections, copperhead holes are interspersed with protection bolts.

If non-piton bolts are placed on first ascents, they should be of the kind that expand from the back of the hole. Conventional contraction bolts, as used in granite, are almost worthless in soft sandstone.

Because of the soft nature of sandstone, pitons scar the rock much faster than they would on granite. Hammers should never be used on routes that are designated hammerless (even to test fixed anchors, as this tends to loosen them) and should be used as little as safety allows on other routes (pitons might still be slotted as nuts).

There has been encouragement in the climbing media for a technique known as "constructive scarring." When a piton must be driven with a hammer, it is placed pointing inwardly down. When it is removed, one does not hammer down on the piton past the horizontal position—in other words, one strongly favors the upward blows over the downward blows. In this way, the resulting scar might eventually permit climbing the route without a hammer. This will certainly make the route an easier aid climb in the long run, but at least the visual blight of ever widening cracks is kept to a minimum. On the other hand, many local climbers would prefer to see normal scarring occur in order to facilitate eventual free climbing efforts. Either way, avoid placing pitons if possible.

Fixed pitons in Zion cracks are often less trustworthy than those in granite. Cracks erode and shift in size, with erosion on southern exposures being greater. Thus, when climbing a new route, it is often best to place a bolt rather than leave a fixed piton; better yet, leave nothing at all.

Local climbers have found that mixing red carpenter's chalk into their white stuff reduces the visual blight of using chalk on Zion's red sandstone. Other climbers find chalk unecessary here.

Descents usually involve rappels—sometimes even of an entire Grade IV or V route. Be prepared to place rappel bolts on new routes and on one pitch climbs, and sometimes to replace or reinforce rappel bolts on established long descents. Extreme care must be taken on descents, as this is where Zion climbing fatalities have occured.

Plenty of water should be carried on long climbs during the warm seasons.

165 foot ropes are necessary on a number of Zion routes.

ENVIRONMENT

While Zion's main canyon is a far cry from being wilderness, the lack of climbers and the verticality of the environment combine to give the climbing an exotic and slightly wild feeling. The tourist-filled road that snakes along the valley floor is somewhat intrusive, but traffic noise is drowned out by river noise, and the views of red sandstone walls lining the canyon's edges is always inspiring. When snow covers the high country just above the canyon rim, the scenery is spectacular in a way that only the Southwest desert can be. Though the desert surrounding Zion Canyon is typically sparce in greenery, the canyon floor is lined with cottonwood and box elder trees, through which the Virgin River flows.

The canyon was produced purely from the carving action of this stream. After a flashflood or during heavy snow melting, the innocuous looking river can turn into a maelstrom, carting off huge hunks of sandstone—and trapping or drowning unwary hikers. During more normal flows, the Virgin River provides a refreshing dip after a hot climb.

Upstream from the road's end, the canyon becomes the "Narrows," a deep chasm that is sometimes only twenty feet wide. A spectacular fifteen mile hike starts outside of the Park and involves hiking in the river and through the Narrows to the road in the main canyon. A permit and a careful check of the weather are required for this hike. Many other spectacular hikes are available, most notably the almost technical "trail" up Angel's Landing (which is also the descent from its routes).

CLIMBING HISTORY

Most of the features in Zion Canyon have biblical names given to them by a missionary in the early 1900's. The Piute Indians had considered the canyon a sacred and fearful place; they refused to stay in the canyon during the darkness of night. Some early climbers also considered the walls intimidating, sometimes more so than those of Yosemite. The first of Zion's major walls to be climbed, The Great White Throne, was not ascended until 1968. By the early 1970's, a number of big routes were being done.

A guide to most of the contemporary long routes was published in the 1972 issue of *Ascent*, but no guidebook has yet been written. Indeed, few magazines have published extensive articles on Zion Canyon. Nevertheless, the place has become known to many in the climbing community.

A few climbers recognized early the destruction that pitons could wreak in the soft rock and began attempting routes exclusively with nuts. With the advent of sophisticated cam nuts in the late 1970's, this method was used wherever possible by an increasing number of climbers. Today, clean climbing should always be stressed.

Though quite a few short routes have been established at Zion, the canyon has always attracted people more for its walls than for its free climbing. This may partially explain why, despite some of the nation's finest climbers having passed through here, few free climbs harder than 5.10 have been established.

CAMPING

Both private and large National Park Service campgrounds are available at the south end of Zion Canyon. The National Park campgrounds ($5) are scenic and near some excellent bouldering. Unfortunately, they can be somewhat congested during late spring weekends and holidays. The private campground is in Springdale, one mile outside of the Park boundary, and offers showers, both for its campers and, for about $2 each, for anyone else.

All the normal conveniences of a small town are also available in Springdale. One local restaurant, the Bit and Spur, has earned high marks in the *New York Times* travel section for its Mexican food. Utah liquor laws have several bizarre quirks, including the fact that one must purchase anything more alcoholic than beer from a Utah State Liquor Store. The restaurant will then provide the "set-up": glasses, mixers, corkscrews—for a fee, of course. There is a liquor store about a mile north of the Bit and Spur. Flanigans Inn has a state liquor store and a decent restaurant.

SEASONS AND WEATHER

Approximate Months	Typical Temperatures High	Low	Likelihood of Precipitation	Frequency of Climbable Days
Dec-Feb	50's	30's −	low	medium
Mar-May	70's	40's	low	very high
Jun-Sep	90's	60's	medium	medium
Oct-Nov	70's −	40's	low	very high

Comments: Summer heat is too much for most climbers. July and August have lots of thundershower activity. Spring and fall temperatures can be wildly variable. Minimal crowds are found during the winter season.

RESTRICTIONS AND WARNINGS

The present park administration has a very open and helpful attitude towards the currently small contingent of climbers visiting the park each year. Visitors are asked to not bring biases and prejudices into their dealings with the Park Service; local climbers hope to preserve the warm and amicable relationship which presently exists.

Because of the relatively few people who have climbed at Zion and the lack of a guidebook, some of the routes in this book have received few, if any, repeat ascents. Descriptions must be followed with special caution and with the attitude that creative route finding may well be needed.

The Park Service no longer requires climbers to register, but it does require backcountry permits for bivouacs.

Navajo Sandstone is often loose and is sometimes unpredictable, especially for those uninitiated to its peculiarities. Read the section on *CLIMBING* for comments on sandstone climbing. For one to two days after a heavy thundershower, the rock can be extremely weak.

The Park Service has not been plagued with a rescue problem, partially due to the high standards of many of those who climb here. This means that they do not have the frequency or experience in rescues that Yosemite National Park does. Also, the nearest hospital is over an hour's drive away. Therefore, despite the ambience of so much tourist traffic on the road below, climbing should be done with the care often reserved for a more remote area.

Fires are permitted in the Park only at developed campgrounds or by backcountry permit.

The weather, though generally fine, can sometimes be severe. Flash-floods can be lethal for those trapped in drainage areas. These floods are especially likely in the late summer when cloudbursts are possible. The summer heat can also be devastating. Winter and early spring can bring sudden cold snaps.

The Great White Thone (not covered in this book) is closed from April 1 to August 31 because of peregrine falcon nesting.

GUIDEBOOKS

There is a looseleaf binder in the Visitor Center that contains first-hand descriptions of routes and climbs. Though many routes are described, many are missing and may never have been written up. Also, the book must be used with caution since often the descriptions are by first ascentionists with no corroboration from other sources.

GUIDE SERVICES AND EQUIPMENT STORES

Presently, there is no Park Service sanctioned climbing guide service for Zion National Park, but they may be revising their policy on special use. The nearest climbing equipment store is in Las Vegas.

EMERGENCY SERVICES

In case of any emergency, contact a Park ranger. In the summer there is a physician's assistant at the Springdale Clinic, located one half mile up Amphitheater Road, which is one half mile south of the South Entrance Station. Regular hours are Wednesdays through Sundays 10 am to 6 pm from May through October (but hours can always change); a doctor is there one day per week, telephone during clinic hours: 772-3226, after hours: 772-3227. Full emergency room facilities are maintained forty-six miles from Zion at the Dixie Medical Center, 544 South 500 East, St. George, telephone: 673-9681. Otherwise, the nearest hospital is in Cedar City, sixty-four miles away from Zion, at the Valley View Medical Center, 595 South 75 East, telephone: 586-6587. Serious cases are sometimes helicoptered to Las Vegas or Salt Lake City.

GETTING THERE

From Cedar City, Color Country Tours (801-586-9916) offers bus transportation three times per week, May to October. Gray Line offers tours from Flagstaff, Arizona. Greyhound and Trailways provide bus service to Cedar City, and Sky West Aviation flies there from Salt Lake City. Hitch-hiking to Zion is not likely to be fast, but might be speeded by wearing a bright climbing rope and shiny carabiners. When standing at the LaVerkin junction, make sure a potential ride is going all the way to Springdale or Zion National Park.

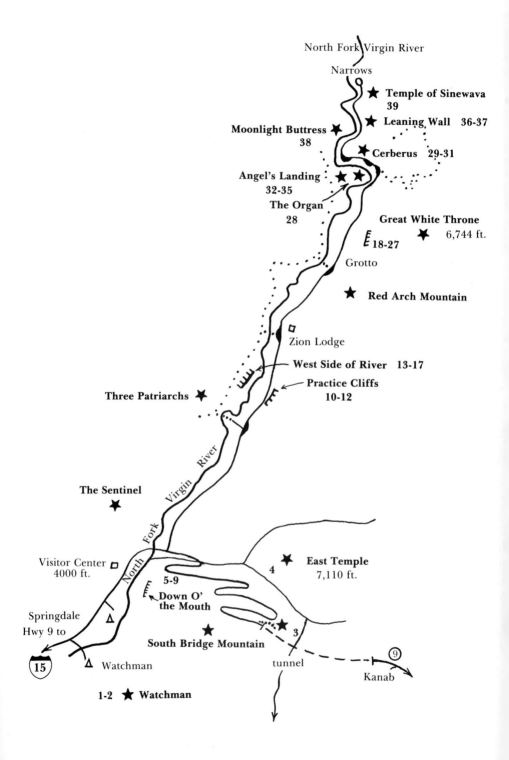

Ron Olevsky on The Headache

Watchman — West Face photo: Dave Jones
Descent: from the top, scramble right and down gully. From **S & M**, either
scramble up choices to top, or down gully to left (via 3rd class and 2-3 rappels)
 1 S & M IV 5.10+ A0 Stacy Austin and Mark Austin, 1984. Exceptionally
clean climbing. Alternating finger cracks and off-widths for 6 long pitches.
One aid move on bolt.
 2 Silmaril V 5.10 A2 Gary Gray and Dave Jones, 1983. On topo, free ratings
in ( ) are estimates by first ascent party who used aid. Gear: standard
sandstone nut rack to 5½", plus 1 LA, 1 long-thick LA, 2 short-thick LA, 1
ea. ½", 2 ea. ⅝", 2 ea. ¾", (After 2nd pitch, need only 2 ea. ⅝".)

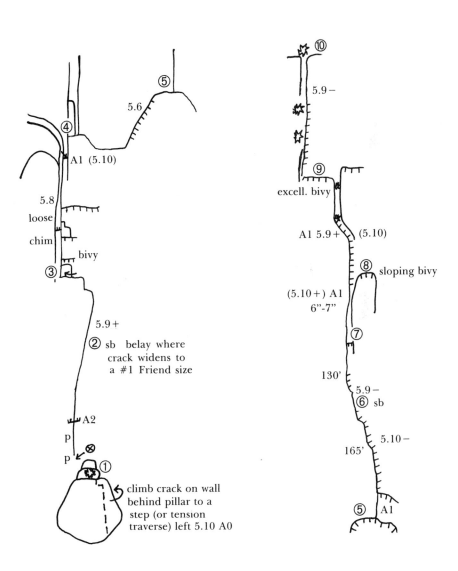

West Face of the Watchman
"The Silmaril" V 5.10 A2

West End Tunnel
3 The Headache III 5.10— Brian Smith and Dana Geary, 1975.

John Harlin and Ron Olevsky on The Headache photo: Adele Hammond

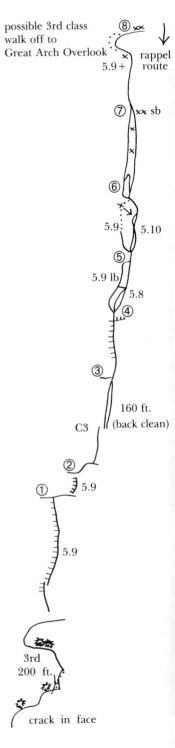

possible 3rd class
walk off to
Great Arch Overlook
⑧ xx ↓
rappel
5.9+   route

⑦ xx sb
x
x

⑥
5.9   5.10

⑤
5.9 lb
5.8
④

③
160 ft.
C3   (back clean)

②
①   5.9

5.9

3rd
200 ft.

crack in face

Southwest Face of East Temple

4 Fang Wall IV-V 5.10 C3 Dave Jones, Mark
Pey, Ron Olevsky and Gary Grey began the
route; completed by Dave Jones and Gary
Grey, 1983. Gear: 2+ sets of Friends, many
small wires for aid, extra ¾"-2" nuts, Tricams,
tube chocks to 6" optional. No pitons. Rappel
the route.

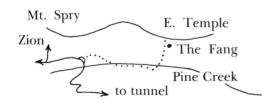

Mt. Spry
Zion
E. Temple
The Fang
Pine Creek
to tunnel

Dave Jones on 1st pitch Empty Pages photo: Mark Pey

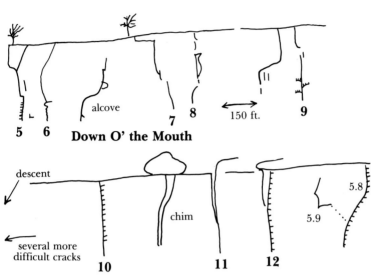

Down O' the Mouth

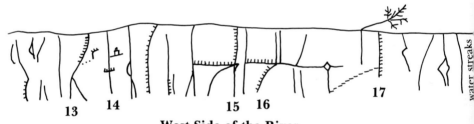

The Practice Cliffs

West Side of the River

Down O' the Mouth
5 Locker 5.8
6 Double Clutch Bulge 5.9+
7 Relapse 5.8
8 Scarface 5.9
9 Blockbuster A2

The Practice Cliffs
10 Lieback 5.9
11 Casual Sex 5.7 classic
12 Hladick 5.9 good

West Side of the River
13 Sandbag 5.8/5.9
14 5.9/5.10
15 Jericho 5.9/5.10 excellent
16 Aton's Chimney 5.10
17 If the Shoe Fits 5.8 worthwhile
Quality of routes is variable. Multiple names possible

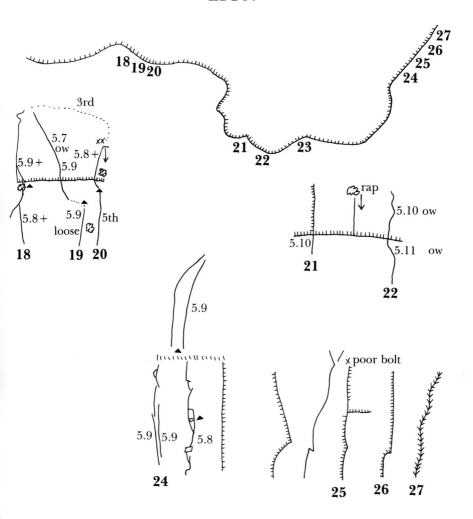

Base of Southwest Face of Great White Throne

Route quality is variable.

18 Rain 5.9+ Jim Beyer and Bob Sullivan, 1979. Nuts to 4", many 2"-3". Sustained, high quality

19 Merced Red 5.9 Jim Beyer and Bob Sullivan, 1979. Nuts to 6", many 2"-3".

20 Box Elder Jam 5.8+ Jim Beyer and Courtney Simkins. Nuts to 4".

21 Crack of REM 5.10 Bob Sullivan and Jim Beyer, 1979.

22 Nemesis 5.11/5.10+ Jim Beyer and Bob Sullivan, 1979. 2 or 3 6" tubes. Possibly Zion's first recorded 5.11.

23 Illusion 5.9 Bob Sullivan and Jim Beyer, 1979. Right hand of 2 face cracks.

24 Twin Cracks 5.9

25 Psychobolt 5.10

26 Grasshopper 5.9

27 Rookie Crack 5.8/5.9 excellent.

The Narrows photo: Ron Olevsky

The Organ – North Side
28 **Organ Grinder 5.9 +** Larr
Derby, Mike Weiss and Bil
Westbay, 1975. Bring several larg
nuts to 4 inches.

Cerberus — South Face
29 **Cave Route 5.7** Jim Dunn, 1970'
30 **Cherry Crack 5.10 (or 5.9?)** Fir:
recorded ascent: Dave Strickle
Tim Forsell and Keith Egertoi
1979. 165 foot rope.
31 **Coconut Corner III 5.10 +** Dav
Breashears and Mike Weiss, 197{
The right facing corner. Brin
nothing smaller than 3", sever;
3"- 4", full set of tube chock
Good bolt belays and rappels.

Cerberus – South Face

Zion bouldering

North Face Angel's Landing   photo: Gary Gray

Descent: Angel's Landing Trail—tricky in the dark!

32 Northeast Buttress IV 5.10+ A1 Randy Aton, Mark Austin and Phil Hancy, 1981. Only about 30 feet of aid. Normal rack plus small wires and/or 6 KB.

33 Lowe Route V 5.8 A2 Jeff Lowe and Cactus Bryan, 1970. Pitches: 1-4) free, up dihedrals and chimneys to a sandy ledge, 5-6) aid to belay on ramp, 7) go left to thin aid crack up overhanging steps to good ledge (bivy potential), 8-10) from right end of ledge, a 4 bolt ladder leads to good crack, up cracks and over one overhang to horizontal fault, 9) face climb up and left into large sloping recess, 10) climb out right side to 2nd recess 200 ft below summit, 11) right out of recess to top. Gear: include some KB's.

34 Angel Hair V 5.8-5.11 A3 FA: Jim Dunn and partner, 1974. The line is obvious, with many free climbing possibilities. Possibly a bit loose. Gear: KB to 6" tube chocks.

35 Empty Pages V 5.9-5.10 A4+ Mark Pey and Dave Jones, 1982. Gear: 1-2 sets brass nuts, 1 set nuts (emphasize smaller sizes), 2 sets friends (emphasize smaller sizes), #1 Tricams useful, hooks (Chouinard, not Leeper), 1 RURP (rurp placement might be destroyed, bring wire to bypass by reaching to bolt), 5 KB (long-thin most useful), 3 LA, 6 ea. ½", 2 ea. ⅝"-¾", 3 ea. ⅜" copperheads for drilled holes.

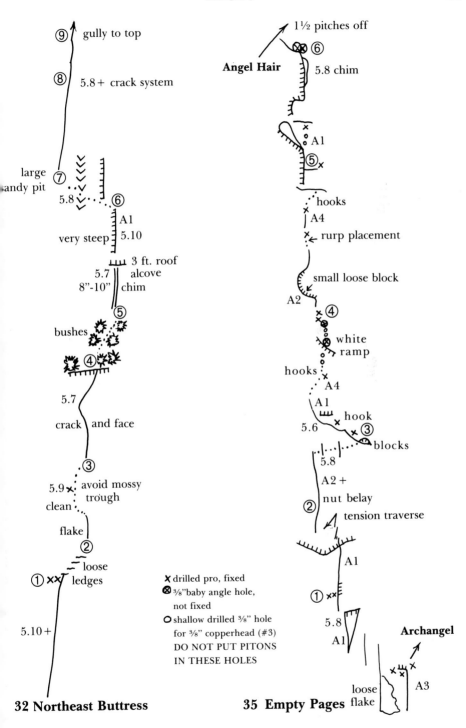

gully to top

1½ pitches off

Angel Hair

5.8 chim

5.8+ crack system

A1

large sandy pit

5.8

very steep

A1
5.10

hooks
A4

rurp placement

3 ft. roof
5.7 alcove
8"-10" chim

small loose block

A2

white
ramp

bushes

hooks

A4

5.7

A1

crack and face

5.6 hook

blocks

5.8

avoid mossy trough

5.9

clean

A2+

nut belay

flake

tension traverse

loose
ledges

A1

X drilled pro, fixed
⊗ ⅜"baby angle hole, not fixed
O shallow drilled ⅜" hole for ⅜" copperhead (#3)
DO NOT PUT PITONS IN THESE HOLES

5.8

5.10+

Archangel

A1

32 Northeast Buttress

35 Empty Pages loose flake

A3

Leaning Wall

Descent: Cross drainage east and rappel from tree past slab, then down and right. Four rappels with excellent ledges to Moonshadow Falls.

36 Equinox V 5.9 A3 or IV 5.10+ Ron Olevsky and Mike Strassman, 1984. FFA: George Allen and Dave Jones, 1984.

37 Space Shot V 5.6 A2 Ron Olevsky and Dave Jones, 1978. Gear: standard aid rack with nuts and friends, small angles for drilled holes, 165 ft rope.

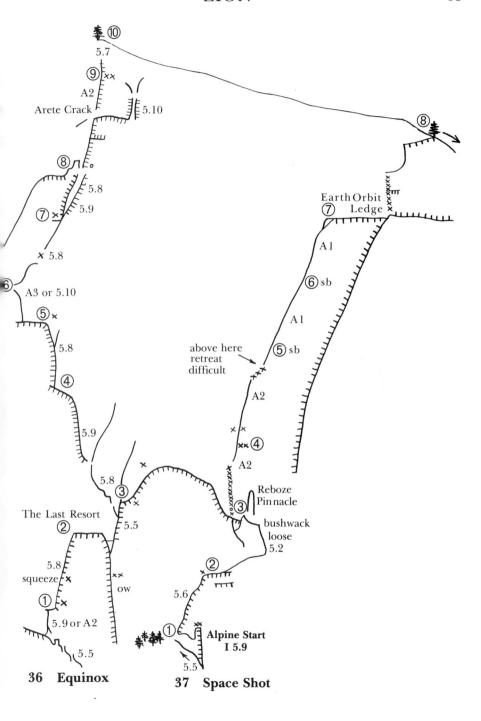

⑩
5.7

⑨ xx
A2
Arete Crack

5.10

⑧ ⨀

5.8

⑦ x

5.9

⑧ 𝄢

x 5.8

⑥
A3 or 5.10

⑤ x

5.8

④

5.9

5.8

The Last Resort
②

5.5

5.8
squeeze x

① x

5.9 or A2

5.5

36 Equinox

Earth Orbit
⑦   Ledge x

A1

⑥ sb

A1

above here
retreat
difficult

⑤ sb

A2

x x

xx ④

A2

Reboze
Pinnacle

③

bushwack
loose
5.2

②

5.6

x

ow

①

Alpine Start
I 5.9

5.5

37 Space Shot

⑧

③

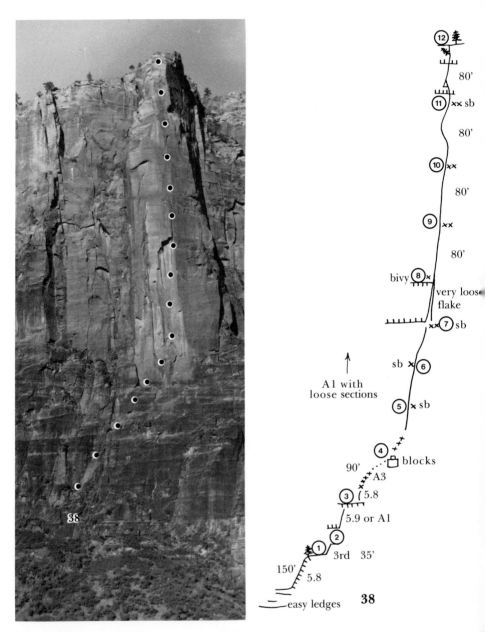

Moonlight Buttress photo: Mark Kelleher
38 Moonlight Buttress V 5.9 A3 Mike Weiss and Jeff Lowe, 1971. Very
popular, but has a some dangerously loose rock. Gear: Multiple sets friends,
Tricams, hooks, KB to 1½" with many ¾"-1" for pitches 4-12. Bring little
over 2½". Use Friends and nuts whenever possible.

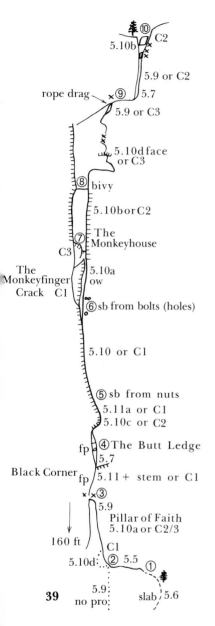

Temple of Sinewava

Descent: Up NW ridge of Observation Point (4th-5.5) then down trail 5½ miles,
or 5 rappels down route.

39 Monkeyfinger Wall V 5.9 C3 or 5.11+ Ron Olevsky and Rob Schnelker,
1978. FFA: Drew Bedford and Pokey Amory, 1984. Goes all nuts, except
small angles for drilled holes. Gear: Small stoppers to 3½" nuts, cams very
useful, keyhole hanger.

Rappelling into Taylor Canyon, Moses behind

CANYONLANDS

HIGHLIGHTS

The Utah desert is a magical place. Starry nights, howling coyotes and quiet solitude are as noteworthy to the visiting climber as the infinite number of cracks that split unlimited expanses of clean red sandstone. Some climbers are drawn to the free standing towers of this region, others to the one or two pitch climbs on canyon walls. Of the uncounted canyons and many spires, three areas have been selected for this book because of their relative popularity: Indian Creek Canyon, Moses Tower, Castleton Tower. The rock is solid as non-metamorphosed sandstone goes, but soft in comparison to granite; blocks can fracture, protection can pull out, and footholds can crumble. Because help for an injured person is a long, long way off, many climbers consider the desert best left for sightseeing. For others, desert climbing will fill a niche like no other place in America.

CLIMBING

The Canyonlands were eroded out of several layers of distinctive sandstone. The most conspicuous bed is that of the Wingate sandstone because its remarkably solid rock cleaves in vertical planes. This layer is 100 to 600 feet thick, and every ten to twenty feet a crack or corner splits most or all of its height. These cracks, ranging in width from fingernail to chimney, are of a uniformity and quality that would make them stand apart even in Yosemite. In fact, it's this uniformity that often makes the climbing so difficult. If the crack is the "wrong" size it's likely to be the wrong size for ten or even fifty feet. This uniformity used to be the bane of desert free climbing. A crack that doesn't taper does a very poor job of holding ordinary nuts, so boldness on the lead was critical for most routes. The advent of camming nuts (e.g. Friends and Tri-Cams) changed that. Now climbs are infinitely more protectable, though one still has to be careful: a long fall onto a Friend (especially a smaller one) can rip it out of the soft sandstone. Even this relatively good sandstone is soft enough that a rope run over an edge will often cut a deep groove.

The three areas chosen for this book are the most popular in the region, mostly because of convenient access. The likelihood of encountering other climbers is relatively high in these places; if true solitude is desired, one needs merely to wander a bit deeper into the Canyonlands—uncounted walls with virgin rock await the explorer.

Indian Creek Canyon, just outside of Canyonlands National Park, features 100 to 300 foot walls with an incredible array of cracks and corners. With a paved road running along the valley floor and less than a hundred yards of talus to climb, access could not be much more convenient. In order to maintain the climbing experience currently enjoyed, no route information from Indian Creek Canyon is included in this guide. Many routes can be spotted by searching for rappel slings (binoculars often help). There are also numerous lines waiting to be climbed. Most routes are rappelled from where they reach the canyon rim or from where the rock quality degenerates. IT IS VITALLY IMPORTANT TO NOT ADD BOLTS TO EXISTING ROUTES! Be sure to search carefully with binoculars for bolts before concluding that yours is an unclimbed line. An increasing number of routes are being climbed without belay bolts; please do not use bolts if they can be safely avoided.

Moses, in Taylor Canyon and within National Park boundaries, is one of the most beautiful of the desert's towers. Aptly named, it has the shape of a robed old man, complete with flowing beard. In the rosy glow of sunrise, the **Primrose Dihedrals** on Moses' southeast side is one of the most strikingly beautiful climbs imaginable. Other routes in the area, including on neighboring Zeus and Wafer spires, also follow aesthetic lines; all routes are three to seven pitches long. With a four wheel drive vehicle or risky two wheel driving, one can make it to within a mile of Moses. Otherwise, access involves up to five miles of walking with a popular option including two rappels into Taylor Canyon.

Unlike other desert spires, which tend to be adjacent to canyon walls Castleton Tower and the nearby Priest and Nuns, dominate their surrounding valley. Perched on a massive talus cone, 500 foot Castleton has become by far the most popular desert climb.

Many famous spire climbs of the Southwest, including Ship Rock Spider Rock, and the Totem Pole are found on Indian reservation land They have not been included in this book because the Indians currentl do not allow climbing on the reservation. While some people sneak onto the spires, this is a violation of the laws of the Navajo and Hopi nations. White encroachment has driven the Native Americans onto a miniscule token of their former lands; respect for tribal wishes on this remaining fraction seems in order.

Bolts should be inspected with special caution in the soft sandstone of the Canyonlands region. Some bolts, usually placed by parties unfamiliar with this rock, will pull out. One quarter inch bolts are almost useless; the most trustworthy bolts are ½ inch angle pitons placed into ⅜ inch drilled holes—these are refered to as "drilled angles." Pitons placed in cracks destroy the rock immediately and become useless in a very short period of time; even the most securely placed piton can usually be pulled out by hand within a few months of weathering.

ENVIRONMENT

Many climbers have spent a lot of time climbing here before they realized that the real allure of the desert lies in its environment, not its routes. The vast spaces, the remoteness, and the desert's simplicity offers a sense of freedom that gets drowned in the confusion of more developed areas.

Even remote mountains somehow lack the grand emptiness of the southwestern desert. Both show the strains of a harsh environment—bare rock, open spaces, weather-beaten plants and rarely seen animals—but in the mountains you can always drop back down to treeline, to cool green, shady places next to rushing streams and maybe huckleberry patches. In the desert there is less escape. Even if the car is only a few miles away, there is no visual retreat from the dry solitude of the desert. What looks like a creek from the top of the climb is often a dry stream bed shimmering in the midday heat. It takes some getting used to.

Castleton Tower feels less remote because civilization is closer and the nearby La Sal Mountains lend scenery of green and white slopes to the many hues of red in the surrounding desert landscape. If one is lucky enough to arrive after a late winter snowstorm, the reds of carved rock are offset by a white blanket covering gentler slopes. Also spectacular under snow is nearby Arches National Park, where a great variety of sandstone arches illustrate the carving action of desert winds.

Ancient human carvings can be seen along many of the walls of Indian Creek Canyon. Indian petroglyphs, some five feet tall, await discovery by those with a keen eye, while Newspaper Rock has been named a historical site because of its concentrated collection of drawings covering a span of several thousand years. Please preserve and respect these artifacts by resisting the urge to climb on them or to touch them—oil from one's fingers contributes to their destruction. It is also illegal to harm these cutural resources in any way—including picking up arrow-heads and pottery shards. Digging around these sites is absolutely forbidden and has been punished by three to five years in Federal prison.

Because of the special beauty and remote wilderness feeling of climb-ing in the Canyonlands region, some people have been reluctant to share the experience with the public. In an attempt to preserve the uniqueness of this special place, all visitors should be especially careful to minimize their impact; this might include not shouting belay signals when other climbers are nearby. While litter is not to be tolerated anywhere, it is especially obnoxious in such a place as this. Please read the *RESTRIC-TIONS AND WARNINGS* section for more suggestions on how to avoid impact on the environment.

CLIMBING HISTORY

Desert climbing began with attempts on Ship Rock, an 1,800 foot volcanic plug in New Mexico. Colorado climbers made attempts in the early 1930's, and soon fame spread nationwide. After an alleged twelve attempts had been made on the rock, a team of Southern California climbers finally succeeded in reaching the summit in 1939. Virtually all other desert spires are sandstone, which at that time was considered too friable to climb. Not until the 1950's did climbers start exploring the many incredible sandstone spires protruding from canyon walls and valley floors. Many of these ascents were made by teams from California though prolific Northwesterners, Coloradans, and even Easterners put in their appearances; Utah had produced few resident climbers by then Castleton may have been the first tower to be climbed (1961) in the Canyonlands area, followed by the Titan (1962) and gradually extending to many of the sundry spires and free-standing pinnacles scattered throughout the vast region. Moses, one of the most aesthetic desert towers, was not climbed until 1972. Moses, like many other towers, was first discovered by air reconnaissance, and then reached by four wheel drive vehicle.

Indian Creek Canyon illustrates a different approach to desert climb-ing. Where previously people had been interested in reaching summits in the early 1970's a few Colorado climbers brought free climbing attitudes to the desert. Here in Indian Creek, they were interested purely in the quality of free climbing in the perfect crack systems. Initially protection was the limiting factor in such climbs, as the parallel-sided cracks refused to accept nuts well and the scarring effects of pitons were anathema to the ethics of these young climbers. The invention of Friends in the late 1970's brought improved (though still not entirely safe) protection to these free climbs. A tradition was imported from the Garden of the Gods of placing bolts, preferably "drilled angles," at belays or wherever a piton would otherwise be considered necessary.

By the later 1970's and 1980's, contemporary free climbing standards were being applied to many desert spires, combining the aesthetics of free climbing with the thrill of reaching a summit. Three aid routes on Moses were freed, several new routes were added to Castleton and nearby spires, and other towers were likewise searched out for first free ascents. Castleton especially, because of its well protected 5.9 route and inclusion in *Fifty Classic Climbs of North America*, became a relatively popular climb during this period, receiving nearly a hundred separate ascents per year.

The publication of this guidebook, the first to cover more than a couple routes in book form, will undoubtably increase traffic in several Canyonlands locales. To some, this is a highly negative impact on a long-cherished "private" haunt. Those who wish complete privacy will be driven to less easily accessible canyons and spires, giving up what was once reached within a stone's throw of a paved road. Climbers are urged to respect the desert experience of others by minimizing their impact in as many ways as possible. Traditions should be respected, including placing the minimum number of bolts on new routes, never adding bolts to old routes (occasional REPLACEMENTS may be necessary), making those bolts drilled angles (never ¼ inch bolts), and not using pitons on free routes (a single placement will forever scar the soft rock).

CAMPING

Camping for desert climbing areas outside of National Park boundaries is a simple affair; pull off the road and set up a tent (or roll out a bivouac sack). Favorite locations can be found near each climbing area. To begin, try camping near the Colorado River for Castleton climbs and at the free campground near Newspaper Rock for Indian Creek climbs.

Do not drive off of established dirt roads since this does immediate long-term damage to the fragile desert vegetation. In the National Park itself, it is illegal to even drive on the shoulder of dirt roads. It is also illegal to build fires except on metal platforms so that the burning embers do not scar the soil. Charcoal should be carried out or buried. No firewood may be gathered within the Park, even if already dead. This is important because dead wood is needed for fertilizing the soil for future generations of struggling desert plants. Please read the *RESTRICTIONS AND WARNINGS* section for more suggestions on minimizing impact on the environment.

Within National Park Boundaries, vehicle campers are required to used designated backcountry vehicle campsites. All other campers are required to use designated backcountry campsites or to camp out of sight and one-half mile from the road corridor and any developed area or trailhead. Camping is not allowed within 100 feet of recognizable archeological or historic sites or within sensitive areas or where it might affect water sources. Camping near Moses is permitted, but a permit is required. Permits may be obtained at any Ranger Station, including headquarters on the main street on the northern edge of Moab and at the Neck (see map).

Water must usually be carried in; local river water must be thoroughly treated if one even has the courage to drink it at all.

The former Uranium mining town of Moab offers coffee shops, beer and ice cream—not to mention less essential items like showers, laundromats, groceries and gas. Numerous river rafting companies are also found here. Many people consider floating through the Canyonlands as the ultimate way to experience its beauty, especially if the weather is too hot to climb.

Nearer to Indian Creek Canyon, Monticello offers similar services.

SEASONS AND WEATHER

Approximate Months	Typical Temperatures		Likelihood of Precipitation	Frequency of Climbable Days
	High	Low		
Dec-Feb	30's +	20's −	very low	low
Mar-May	70's +	40's −	low	very high
Jun-Sep	90's	70's	low	medium
Oct-Nov	70's −	40's	very low	very high

Comments: Spring can provide extremely variable weather, sometimes with high winds accompanying storms.

RESTRICTIONS AND WARNINGS

Climbing in the desert is completely unlike any other climbing experience. Self sufficiency is the key. Sufficient water, sufficient skill with one's car on dirt roads, sufficient bolts to replace old ones or ensure safety on new routes, sufficient climbing knowledge not to get into trouble, and possibly, sufficient first aid skills to get out of trouble. The nearest hospital is usually many miles away, and rescues would be slow to come by. In fact, it could be weeks before anyone discovered that a climbing party was in trouble on a remote tower. The rock is often loose, protection frequently unreliable, and climbing difficult. These factors must be counterbalanced against the beauty of the routes. For many it is better to simply hike and explore this region than to risk the hazards of climbing here.

Another special hazard is the danger of flash floods in dry washes. Be sure not to camp in such spots.

Registration for camping near Moses is required by the National Park Service, and a backcountry permit is required for any route within Park boundaries (in this guide, Moses). This can be done at any Ranger Station.

Most of the legal and moral restrictions in the Canyonlands involve minimizing impact on the fragile desert environment. The Park Service issues pamphlets with many suggestions: keep vehicles on the roads and feet on the trails—much of the ground contains micro-plant life that is scarred by foot prints and can take a decade to recover (this soil is called "cryptogamic soil" and is recognized by its darker brown color); carry out every scrap of litter; follow the camping suggestions in the Camping section; wash dishes, clothes, etcetera at least 100 feet from water sources; bury excrement and paper at least six inches deep in soil (not sand) and at least 100 feet from trails and water sources; do not touch or remove artifacts; do not add any markings to the rocks. In other words, leave the environment in at least as good shape as you found it. If done well, no one should ever know that you were there.

To preserve the desert experience for others, please avoid making excessive noise when other people are around. This includes minimizing the shouting of belay signals.

In 1984, the National Park Service identified the following rules for climbing within Canyonlands and Arches National Parks and Natural Bridges National Monument:

1   Each climbing party must obtain a backcountry permit from a park official and identify climbing plans prior to the climb. Free permits are available at Park Service office buildings in Moab and Monticello and at visitor centers or ranger stations within the Parks or Monument.

2   Areas may be closed to climbing for natural resource protection. Climbing will be prohibited any place where spectators gather to view a climb which will create a safety hazard.

3   The entire Salt Creek Archeological District is closed to rock climbing.
4   All climbers are encouraged to abide by a clean-climbing ethic.
5   The following features are closed to climbing: **a.** Any arch or natural bridge found on the United States Geological Survey Topographical map (Washer Woman in the Island-in-the-Sky district is an exception and is open to climbing). **b.** Arches N.P.: Balanced Rock, Three Penguins. **c.** Natural Bridges: Sphinx Rock. **d.** The Confluence Overlook in Needles. **e.** Airport Towers, Island-in-the Sky district, is closed to climbing from March 1 to June 30, yearly. This is identified as an endangered species critical resource area.

GUIDEBOOKS
Fifty Classic Climbs of North America (1979) by Steve Roper and Allen Steck. This book covers one route on Castleton Tower and one on the Titan. Published by the Sierra Club, 530 Bush Street, San Francisco, CA 94108. Several hiking guidebooks exist to the area, including *Canyon Country Hiking* (1977) by F.A. Barnes. Published by Wasatch Publishers Inc., 4647 Idlewild Road, Salt Lake City, UT 84117.

GUIDE SERVICES AND EQUIPMENT STORES
Rim Cyclery at 94 W. 100 N., in Moab has a limited supply of climbing equipment. Grand Junction, 100 miles northeast of the Canyonlands, is the nearest source for a more complete selection of gear. Some climbing guides from various states will provide custom guiding in the Canyonlands.

EMERGENCY SERVICES
In an emergency, contact the National Park rangers for the Moses area for Castleton call the Grand County Sheriff in Moab at 259-8115; for Indian Creek Canyon call the San Juan County Sheriff in Monticello at 587-2237. The hospital in Moab is the Allen Memorial Hospital, 719 West 4th South, telephone: 259-7191; the hospital in Monticello is San Juan County Hospital, 384 West 300 North, telephone 587-2116.

Other National Park phone numbers include:
Island-in-the-Sky Ranger Station (Moses): 259-6577
Needles Ranger Station (near Indian Creek Canyon): 259-6568
Maze Ranger Station:259-6513   NPS Monticello Office:587-2737
NPS Moab Office:259-7164   Arches National Park:259-8161

GETTING THERE
Trailways buses serve Monticello and Moab, and Alpine Aviation provides air service from Salt Lake City to Moab, from which cars may be rented. Hitch hiking is likely to be slow.

Hidetaka Suzuki on Supercrack

CANYONLANDS

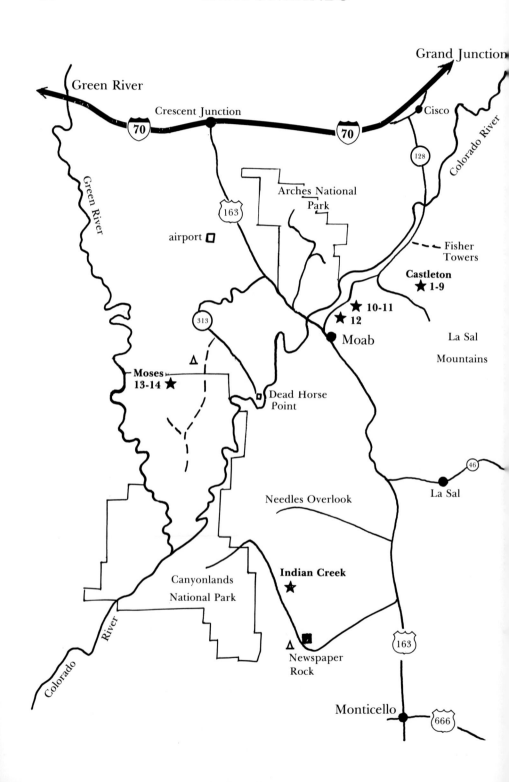

Grand Junction

Green River

Crescent Junction

70   **70**

Cisco

128

Green River

Arches National
Park

163

airport ▢

Fisher
Towers

Castleton
★ **1-9**

★ **10-11**
★ **12**

● **Moab**

La Sal

Mountains

313

△

Moses
13-14 ★

▢ **Dead Horse**
Point

Colorado River

46

● **La Sal**

Needles Overlook

Indian Creek
★

Canyonlands

National Park

△ ▣
Newspaper
Rock

163

Colorado River

Monticello ● 666

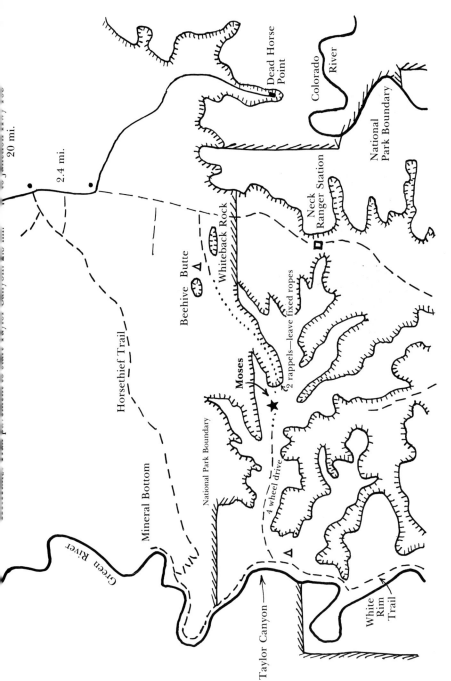

20 mi.

2.4 mi.

Dead Horse Point

Colorado River

National Park Boundary

Neck Ranger Station

Whiteback Rock

Beehive Butte

Horsethief Trail

Moses

2 rappels—leave fixed ropes

Moses Access

Mineral Bottom

National Park Boundary

4 wheel drive

Green River

Taylor Canyon →

White Rim Trail

Castleton Area

Descents: From the Nuns, two rappels from the far northern end are required. Finding the first rappel anchors requires considerable searching; very long slings should be left to prevent the ropes from jamming. The second rappel is about 170 feet long.

From Castleton, the standard descent is to rappel the **Kor-Ingalls Route** (#5). If congested with climbers, extreme care should be taken to not dislodge rocks.

Priest

1 West Side III 5.10 (or 5.9 C1) Layton Kor, Fred Beckey and Harvey T. Carter, 1962. FFA:Jeff Achey and Chip Chace 1981. Runout squeeze chimney first pitch. A classic desert climb.

Variation - 1ˢᵗ pitch on east side, then traverse (tunnel!) through chimney

5.9

5.11

5.10

5.10

2

Nuns

2 Crack Wars III 5.11 Charlie Fowler and Glenn Randall 1983. Several large nuts to 4 inches. No bolts at belays. Crystalline (painful) crack.

Nuns
3 Fine Jade III 5.11 Chip Chace and Pat Ellingwood, 1984.

Castleton West Face
4 West Face III 5.10+

Castleton South Face

√ **5 Kor-Ingals III 5.9 −** Layton Kor and Huntley Ingalls, 1961. FFA: Chuck Pratt and Steve Roper, 1963. The most popular route in the desert.

6 Arrowhead-Left Side II 5.10 Ed Webster and Chester Dreiman, 1982.

7 Stardust Cowboy III 5.11 A1 Ed Webster and Chester Dreiman, 1982.

Castleton North Face

8 Northeast Chimney III 5.8 (or harder?) Offwidth.

9 North Face III 5.11 FA: French party, 1973. FFA: Ed Webster and Buck Norden, 1979. Finest route on Castleton.

Chip Chace and Charlie Fowler on Pale Fire, Moses

Along the Colorado River
10 Peapod Crack 5.10 Rope jams easily.

Along the Colorado River
11 Last Supper 5.10+ Bad protection to start route (tiny wires) on 5.10 climbing. Descent: deep in the canyon to the left, with rappels next to beautiful waterfalls.

Along the Colorado River
12 Sorcerer's Apprentice 5.10 A desert classic. Descent: 2 rappels from bolts on left side.

Moses and neighbors from the northwest

Hidetaka Suzuki on last pitch Moses, Zeus in background

Hidetaka Suzuki on 4th pitch Primrose Dihedrals

5.8

5.9

The Ear

5.11

5.9+

5.10+

5.10 −

5.10

13   5.11

Moses South Face
13 Primrose Dihedrals IV 5.10 C1 or 5.11 Ed Webster solo, 1979. FFA: Ed Webster and Steve Hong, 1979. One of the finest routes in the desert.

Moses North Face

14 North Face (Pale Fire free) IV 5.9 C3 or 5.12 Fred Beckey, Eric Bjornstad, Jim Gavin, Thom Nephew and Greg Markov, 1972. FFA: Chip Chace and Charlie Fowler, 1981. As a free climb, the upper route diverges from the bolt ladder and is poorly protected on 5.11 face climbing.

Ophir Wall

TELLURIDE

HIGHLIGHTS

Telluride is a small historic mining town in a spectacular mountain setting. Tucked away up a high alpine valley, the town is home to music, wine, dance, and film festivals—including a mountaineering film festival. Its nearby hiking, skiing, frozen waterfall and crag climbing make the town a mountaineer's heaven. The area's best cliffs are actually ten miles west of town at the small communities of Ophir and Ames. The Ophir Wall and neighboring Cracked Canyon are included in this book because they are the best developed crags in the region. Heavily fractured, this granitic rock provides many excellent crack and face routes between one and six pitches in length. As long as people continue to maintain some discretion, beautiful free camping abounds as well.

CLIMBING

The main cliff at the Ophir Wall is steep and a full 650 feet tall. The routes meander to connect discontinuous cracks, avoid overhangs, and find belay ledges. The granite here is fractured into irregular patterns and is not always solid; route finding skills and delicacy on unstable rock can be important on some climbs. Getting to the cliff, on the other hand, is no problem at all: a virtual hop, skip and a jump up the small talus field and one is on the rock.

It takes a few more jumps to get up the talus field to neighboring Cracked Canyon, but the concentration of one pitch routes on very solid granite make the short walk well worthwhile. As the name implies, the narrow canyon is split by a multitude of cracks of all sizes. While some good face climbs exist here, cracks are definitely the mainstay of the canyon. Do be careful walking on the steep canyon floor; the talus is very unstable and rocks can easily be rolled onto people lower down. For this reason, some people prefer to rappel the route instead of using the 3rd class descent higher in the canyon.

The Ames Wall, just down-valley from the Ophir Wall, is famous for its winter waterfall ice climbing (as is Telluride for Bridalveil Falls, the highest frozen waterfall in Colorado). It does also have many excellent rock climbs which are slightly less popular than those at the Ophir Wall.

Several good bouldering areas exist in the region, including the Idorado Boulders near Bridalvail Falls and Society Turn, the turnoff for Ophir just outside of Telluride. The Society Turn climbs are sheltered by overhangs and offer good climbing when it is raining or snowing elsewhere.

ENVIRONMENT

With the San Juan mountains precipitously rising on three sides, Telluride has been described as "the most amazing town site in America." Because of its mining heritage, the town is a National Historic District. Among Colorado ski resort towns, it has thus far avoided massive development and exploitation, in part because it lacks an airport. This is bound to change soon.

The next valley west, around Ophir, is also stunningly beautiful. Views from the cliff extend from snow capped mountains and forested valleys to the Ames Wall, with its ribbon-like waterfall. While the climbing cliffs are granite, many of the nearby mountain sides are decomposing sedimentary rock filled with enough iron to give them a painted red appearance. The pale green of budding aspen set against this red background, is rivalled in beauty only by the incredible colors of the same leaves preparing to drop in the fall. Because of its high altitude—almost 9,000 feet—this area retains moderate temperatures and a splendid display of flowers throughout the summer.

The vertical relief of the San Juans make them perhaps the most spectacular mountains in Colorado—in the heart of the southern portions of the mountains there are even rock faces to rival those of Rocky Mountain National Park. Since they also receive massive amounts of snow in the winter, the peaks retain a blanket of snow late into the summer season. Avalanche danger from the quantity of snow and long steep slopes make these mountains dangerous for extensive winter touring, but in late spring, these same avalanche chutes build up deep corn snow and become Colorado's finest spring skiing. The region is also filled with streams, many of which offer good fishing.

Telluride itself figures prominently among frontier mining towns, and the residents have been careful to maintain something of the original architecture. This sense of aesthetics shows in the many art festivals hosted in Telluride each summer. In fact, climbers with a cultural bent might end up bagging more ballets and bluegrass shows than routes.

CLIMBING HISTORY

Telluride is rich in history—including the launching of Butch Cassidy's career in bank robbery—but its era of rock climbing is brief. Even though nearby Lizard Head peak was one of the first technical rock climbs in the United States (1920) and the hardest of its day, recorded CRAG climbing did not begin until the early 1970's. Locals occasionally ventured on the rocks, but were often spurred to first ascents in anticipation of visits from famous climbers; locals were afraid of losing all of their best routes to the foreigners. While their illustrious visitors were present, many more good routes were climbed, only to have the cliffs fall back into disuse afterwards. Rockcraft, a well known climbing school from California, was temporarily based in Telluride, but it too faded away. In the 1980's a small number of locals climb regularly in the area, but the largest crowds come with the influx of visitors during the Memorial Day weekend Mountain Film Festival. Leading climbers from around the country—and sometimes the world—gather to watch films at night and recreate on the cliffs during the day.

CAMPING

The region abounds in both official campgrounds and unofficial campsites. If budget is a priority, check out places several miles down the dirt road running from Ophir to Ilium. Please use discretion in choosing sites and in camping practices so as not to endanger having this area closed to camping.The nearby Forest Service fee campground (Sunshine) is just as convenient and has water. There is also a public pay campground on the southeast corner of Telluride, within city limits and an easy walk to town. Naturally, many hotels are also available in town, as are stores, laundry facilities, movies, et cetera.

SEASONS AND WEATHER

Approximate Months	Typical Temperatures		Likelihood of Precipitation	Frequency of Climbable Days
	High	Low		
Nov-Apr	40's −	10's −	high	very low
May-Jun	60's +	30's	medium	high
Jul-Aug	70's +	50's	low-med	very high
Sep-Oct	60's	30's	medium	high

RESTRICTIONS AND WARNINGS

Just below the Ophir Wall is a private residence and private property. Please walk around this land instead of over it. Also be very careful in the Cracked Canyon not to start rock slides when people are below. Drinking the river water, even if treated, is not recommended because of contaminants from mining tailings upstream. The best water near the cliffs is the small stream that flows under the Ophir Road about 100 yards west of the tiny Ophir Post Office.

GUIDEBOOKS

The only guidebook ever published to Telluride rock climbing is long out of print. However, there is a copy available for perusal at Olympic Sports in Telluride. *Telluride Rock: an interim guide* (1978) by Bill Kees.

GUIDE SERVICES AND EQUIPMENT STORES

Olympic Sports, 101 W. Colorado (main street) offers a small collection of climbing equipment, as does Telluride Sports, 226 West Colorado. The locally based guide service is Beyond the Abyss, P.O. Box 952, Telluride, CO 81435, telephone: 303-728-3705.

EMERGENCY SERVICES

In any emergency, contact the San Miguel County Sheriff at 728-3931. The nearest medical service is in Telluride: Mountain Medical Services, 500 W. Pacific, 728-3848.

GETTING THERE

No public transportation serves Ophir itself, though one can hire a taxi in Telluride. Trailways bus lines goes to Telluride, and shuttle service is available with Telluride Transit from the airport in Montrose. Reservations are required 24 hours in advance.

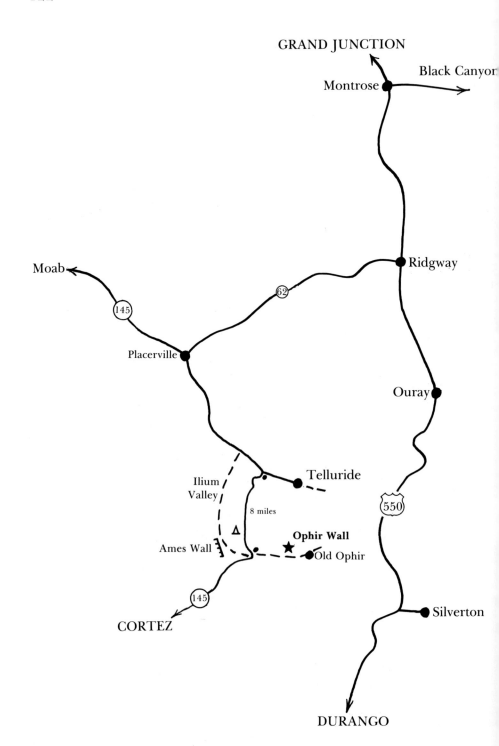

Ophir Wall and Cracked Canyon

Old Ophir Town Hall   photo: Marilyn Harlin

Ace Kvale on Powder in the Sky photo: Antoine Savelli

Adele Hammond on Dog Leg

Ophir Wall

1 **Dr. Gizmo III 5.10d** John Long and Lynn Hill, 1980. Extra small to medium nuts.

2 **Emotional Rescue III 5.10b** Bill Kees and Barry Rugo, 1982.

3 **Hot Wee Wee III 5.9** Henry Barber and partner, 1973. Full rack. 5 pitches.

4 **Hidden Secrets III 5.9** Bill Kees and Doug Jones, 1980.

5 **Honey Pot (Left Y-Crack) III 5.10b** Greg Davis and Budge Hirke, 1973 or 1974 for route following Right Y-Crack (5.10), Ace Brown and Dan Langmade for Left Y-Crack. 5-6 pitches.

6 **Post Office Crack III 5.8** The first route done on the cliff (FA unknown). Climbing not especially good. On upper pitches angle left towards large coniferous tree. Four pitches.

7 **Powder in the Sky II 5.10c** Antoine Savelli, Teri Kane and Ace Kvale 1983.

8 **Batman's Delight II 5.9** Tim Kudo, Bill Kees and Jim Gribin 1978.

9 **Ophir Broke II 5.12c** Dan Langmade and Bill Kees, 1976. FFA: John Long and Lynn Hill.

Beginner's Luck photo: Adele Hammond

Lower East Buttress

0 Sweet RP's II 5.11b Antoine Savelli and Teri Kane, 1984. Two pitches.

1 Yorky's Crumpet II 5.8 Bob Sullivan and partner, 1975.

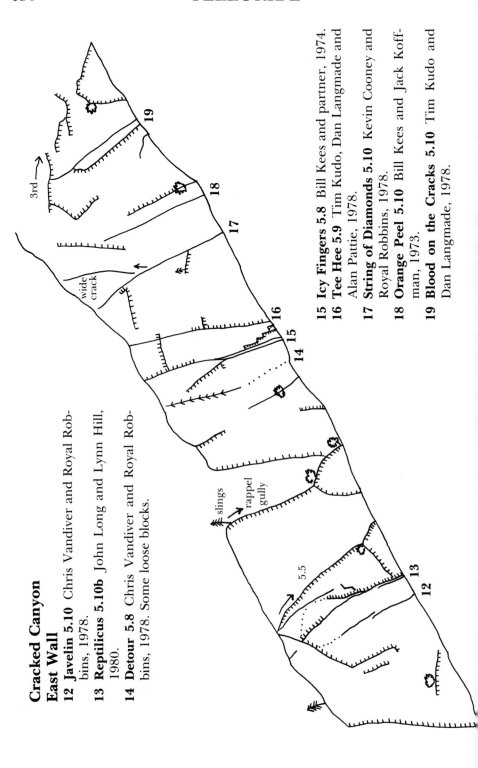

Cracked Canyon
East Wall

12 **Javelin 5.10** Chris Vandiver and Royal Robbins, 1978.

13 **Reptilicus 5.10b** John Long and Lynn Hill, 1980.

14 **Detour 5.8** Chris Vandiver and Royal Robbins, 1978. Some loose blocks.

15 **Icy Fingers 5.8** Bill Kees and partner, 1974.

16 **Tee Hee 5.9** Tim Kudo, Dan Langmade and Alan Pattie, 1978.

17 **String of Diamonds 5.10** Kevin Cooney and Royal Robbins, 1978.

18 **Orange Peel 5.10** Bill Kees and Jack Koffman, 1973.

19 **Blood on the Cracks 5.10** Tim Kudo and Dan Langmade, 1978.

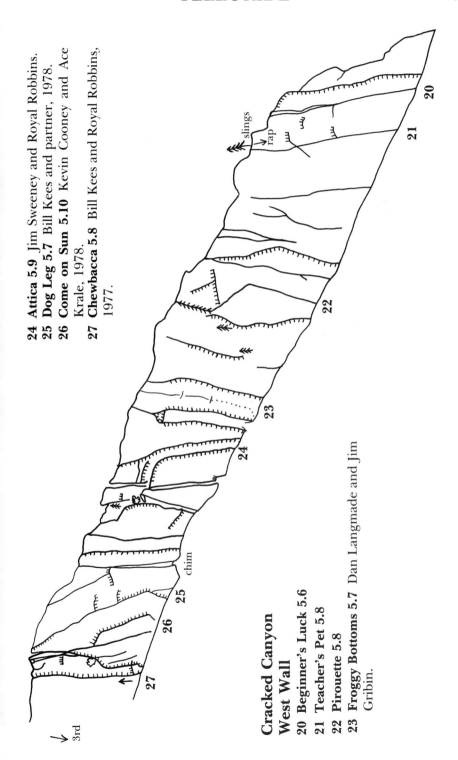

24 **Attica 5.9** Jim Sweeney and Royal Robbins.

25 **Dog Leg 5.7** Bill Kees and partner, 1978.

26 **Come on Sun 5.10** Kevin Cooney and Ace Krale, 1978.

27 **Chewbacca 5.8** Bill Kees and Royal Robbins, 1977.

**Cracked Canyon
West Wall**

20 **Beginner's Luck 5.6**

21 **Teacher's Pet 5.8**

22 **Pirouette 5.8**

23 **Froggy Bottoms 5.7** Dan Langmade and Jim Gribin.

The Black Canyon of the Gunnison

BLACK CANYON

HIGHLIGHTS

The Black Canyon of the Gunnison River is a forbidding place: absolutely vertical cliffs 1,700 to 2,700 feet in height are carved into a chasm as narrow as 1,100 feet across. Sunlight sometimes only barely touches the lower walls, and when it does touch them, it reveals dark granite, laced with rotten pegmatite bands. The climbing is frequently very serious in nature, sometimes on bad rock, with bad protection, long runouts and long, hard routes. This, coupled with poor rescue facilities, makes the Black Canyon a place for only very experienced climbers who can move quickly and safely on difficult ground and are able to effect their own rescue, should the need arise. All the same, the competent climber is rewarded with Colorado's largest walls and some of North America's most astounding climbs.

CLIMBING

Black Canyon granite is extremely variable in quality, ranging from perfectly solid to completely rotten. While most routes follow long crack systems, almost all include sections of face climbing on rough-cut edges. Most notable, however, are the pegmatite bands that are both decomposed and without adequate protection; almost all routes have at least a sampling of this delightful Black Canyon treat. On a number of routes (though few in this book), the protection is not only widely spaced and of questionable quality, but belay anchors can be poor as well. Even routes that minimize these notorious characteristics are made serious by the lack of a ready rescue.

Climbs have been done on both sides of the canyon throughout the several miles that comprise the main chasm of the Black. Nevertheless, the vast majority of attention goes to the 1,700 foot South Face of North Chasm View Wall. This cliff has some of the best rock in the Black, and is conveniently located beneath the campground. Though the Cruise Gully descent to the base of the wall is not especially difficult, it is the subject of many epic tales—especially by those who have had to retreat back up it. Facing south, this cliff receives considerable sunshine; the attendant disadvantage is that dehydration is more of a problem.

Free climbs in the Black are traditionally done in one day in order to minimize hauling. The earliest climbers here began the tradition of climbing light and quickly, even on aid routes. Of course, epics resulting from underestimating time requirements and water consumption are common.

Just down the canyon from Chasm View is the Painted Wall. At about 2,500 feet, it is the largest unbroken cliff in Colorado (and possibly in the Rocky Mountain region). Very few routes pierce its rotten face because this cliff exceeds even Black Canyon standards of risk. Because few climbers are likely to attempt the Painted Wall until they have already built up familiarity with local climbing, no routes from it are described in this book.

Aid routes have not been included because climbers rarely do them on first visits to the Black Canyon. Descriptions for routes throughout the Black can be located in the collection of first-hand topos kept at the North Rim Ranger Station in the summer and at the South Rim Ranger Station at other times.

Despite the long drive separating the North and South Rims, it can prove very rewarding to visit the South Rim first. From there, one can inspect the cliffs (binoculars help for details) and get a better impression of the cliffs one is about to tackle.

ENVIRONMENT

Though other canyons in America may be deeper or narrower, perhaps none combine depth with narrowness and sheer verticality to the extreme that the Black does. These characteristics tend to give the canyon a somber aspect—especially to a climber about to launch onto one of the walls—but they also make this a spectacularly beautiful place.

While approaching the canyon, one drives through gently rolling terrain and it is impossible to tell that a giant chasm has been cleaved between the viewer and the nearby hill. Desert scrub, gnarled pinon pines, and juniper trees cover the canyon rim (at 8,000 feet elevation), but the canyon floor is so dark that little vegetation is found. Still, fish thrive in the Gunnison's waters, attracting fishermen from throughout North America who struggle down, then back up access gullies in pursuit of the plentiful large trout.

CLIMBING HISTORY

In 1541 a Spanish party searched the area for the fabled Seven Cities of Cibola. Though they left disappointed, almost 400 years later (1933) the Black Canyon of the Gunnison was honored with designation as a National Monument for its outstanding scenic qualities. To early North American climbers, the Black would seem the antithesis to what climbing meant: summitless rock walls were approached from the top, by climbing down.

Surprisingly, the Black Canyon was actively climbed by the "San Juan Mountaineers" during the 1930's. Never excelling at technical difficulty, they nevertheless climbed a number of ribs and spires in the canyon.

The Black Canyon fell into obscurity until 1960 when the first major route was done, on South Chasm View Wall. The lead climber was overwhelmed by the fact that Colorado actually had cliffs that could compare in magnitude with those of Yosemite, and in the following five years he made a number of ascents of many of the largest cliffs, including the South Face of North Chasm View. The main face of the Painted Wall, however, resisted all attempts until 1972 when two routes were put up, one of which took nine days in the ascending.

Both of these Painted Wall routes involved considerable hard aid climbing, but in 1982 they were linked together to yield a 30 pitch free route whose first ascent was accomplished in a single day (after several aborted attempts). **Stratosfear** epitomizes the extremes of free climbing in the Black Canyon: unprotected loose pitches, devious route finding on 5.ll+ ground with the occasional fixed copperhead for protection, all done with maximum speed and minimal equipment. In recent years a few new aid routes have been climbed that are extreme in both aid and free climbing difficulty.

Since only the best climbers of their day have generally taken to the Black Canyon, the standards are often commensurate. As an example of the attitudes that a few of the Black's leading climbers hold, one of the first completely free ascents the **Scenic Cruise** (5.10+, 1,700 feet) was made solo in an hour and twenty minutes.

CAMPING

The traditional climber's tenting area is the North Chasm View Campground, just a few yards away from the top of the climbing. It is cheap ($3; free out of season—but also often closed and buried in snow). Since water must be trucked in, campers are urged to be sparing in its use. Also, there is little available firewood, requiring campers to import from outside the Monument whatever is needed. Additional water, food, gasoline and other amenities can be found fourteen miles north in the town of Crawford.

SEASONS AND WEATHER

Approximate Months	Typical Temperatures High	Low	Likelihood of Precipitation	Frequency of Climbable Days
Nov-Apr	30's −	0's	medium	very low
May-Jun	60's +	30's	med-low	med-high
Jul-Aug	90's	50's	low	medium
Sep-Oct	70's −	40's	low-med	high

Comments: The weather in the Black Canyon is extremely variable, especially in the spring and fall. In the summer, the temperatures on the north side are often considered excessive for difficult climbing.

RESTRICTIONS AND WARNINGS

Climbers should check with the North Rim Ranger Station to see if registration is needed before climbing. The canyon floor and approach gullies are often thick with poison ivy. The other dangers of climbing here have already been covered—don't get hurt!

GUIDEBOOKS
No guidebooks exist to the Black Canyon. First-hand topos are available at the North Rim Ranger Station in the summer and at the South Rim at other times.

GUIDE SERVICES AND EQUIPMENT STORES
The nearest equipment stores are in Gunnison and Montrose.

EMERGENCY SERVICES
In case of emergency, contact the North Rim park ranger. If he is not available, call the Montrose County Sheriff at 874-9734. The town of Delta has a hospital: Delta County Memorial Hospital, 100 Stafford, 874-7681.

GETTING THERE
No public transportation serves Black Canyon National Monument and hitch hiking is likely to be slow. Trailways buses and airlines serve Montrose and Delta, from which a car can be rented.

DISTANCES
Crawford – North Rim: 14 mi.
Delta – Crawford: 30 mi.
Gunnison – Crawford: 70 mi.
Hwy 50 – South Rim: 7 mi.
Montrose – Hwy 50: 8 mi.

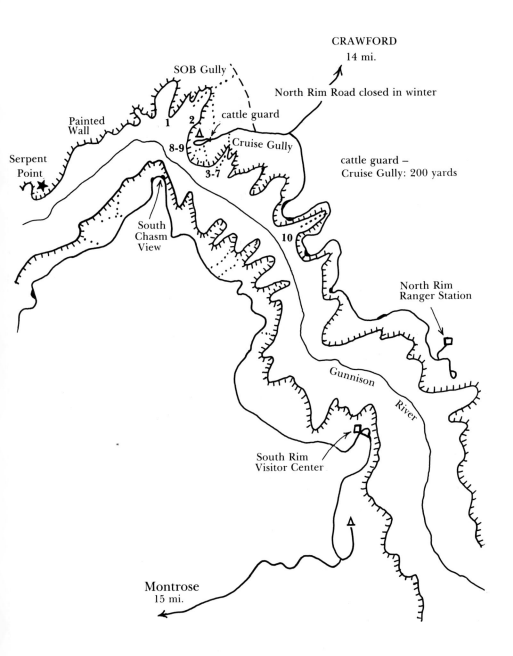

CRAWFORD
14 mi.

SOB Gully

North Rim Road closed in winter

Painted
Wall

cattle guard

1 2

Cruise Gully

8-9

cattle guard –
Cruise Gully: 200 yards

Serpent
Point

3-7

South
Chasm
View

10

North Rim
Ranger Station

Gunnison
River

South Rim
Visitor Center

Montrose
15 mi.

The Russian Arete

The Painted Wall, showing Stratosfear

1 **Russian Arete III 5.9** Layton Kor and Dorworth, mid 1960's. Much offwidth climbing and bad rock, but still a classic.

2 **Escape Artist IV 5.11 or 5.9+** Ed Webster and Chester Dreiman 1982. The climb is on the 3rd major buttress on the left while descending SOB Gully. A prominent left-leaning crack system crosses the front of the buttress to a dihedral system. Approach from the right, then climb 2 stacked blocks below the left-leaning crack. Pitches: 1) climb the right of 2 finger/hand cracks, then move left to a stance (5.9), 2) undercling crack left for 75 ft to ledge (Vector Traverse, 5.9), 3) ascend the dihedral system for 175 ft to ledge on left with fixed piton (5.9), 4) double finger cracks lead to a ledge on the right with fixed piton (5.8), 5) climb easier rock to the left or overhanging finger/hand crack (5.11), 6-8) up slabs (5.5), 9) 120 ft left to top of island. Descent: 150 ft rappel, then up gully. Friends useful on Vector Traverse.

North Chasm View Wall – South Face

North Chasm View Wall
South Face

3 Leisure Climb II 5.9 − Ed Webster and Chester Dreiman, 1982. Start on a grassy ledge 40 ft up. Pitches: 1) climb right-facing corner past bushes to long, narrow ledge on left (5.8), 2) up the left-facing corner, then hand cracks to easy flakes right to good stance, 3) traverse left on ledges, then up flake and over small overlap with thin vertical crack to ledge (5.9 −), 4) climb left-leaning groove to pedestal, ascend outside corner, step right to horn (5.5), 5) chimney to large ledge (5.4), 6) walk left to 5.3 slab.

4 Journey Home IV 5.10 Ed Webster and Brian Becker, 1977. Serious runout on 1st pitch; otherwise excellent protection. Nuts to 3½ in.

5 Scenic Cruise V 5.10 + Ed Webster and Joe Kaelin, 1979. Avoids Cruise offwidth, but 7th pitch traverse is notoriously tricky—off route can be very runout. Possibly most popular long route in the Black Canyon.

6 The Cruise V 5.10 + Layton Kor and Larry Dalke, 1964. FFA: Earl Wiggins and Jim Dunn, 1976. Bring nuts to 4 in.

7 Goss-Logan V 5.11 − Wayne Goss and Jim Logan, 1972. FFA: Leonard Coyne and Ed Russell, 1978. Runout on 7th pitch.

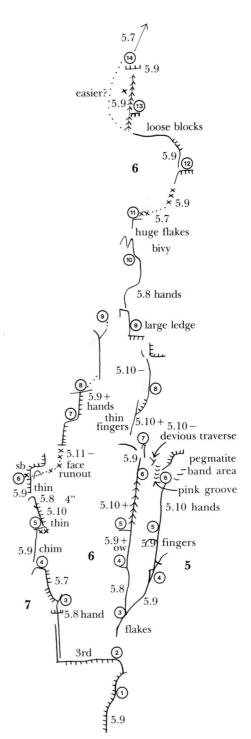

North Chasm View Wall – West Face

North Chasm View Wall
West Face

Notes: For routes 8 and 9 bring tube chocks to #6, large Tri Cams, LA and KB. The degree of seriousness is reduced if a friend is left on the rim with several ropes to lower down (with junars) in case escape is needed.

8 Air Voyage V 5.11+ FFA: Leonard Coyne and Ken Sims, 1980.

9 8th Voyage V 5.11+ FA: Jim Dunn and Dean Tschappet. FFA: Jim Dunn and Leonard Coyne, 1981.

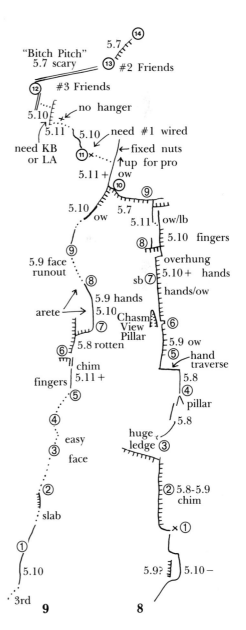

Leonard Coyne on Air Voyage photo: Glenn Randall

Tourist Route from South Chasm View.
10 Tourist Route III 5.8 Ken Trout and Bill Dobbins, 1977.

The Roaring Fork River and the Grotto Cliffs

ASPEN

HIGHLIGHTS

Aspen's fame derives from an affluent lifestyle in which few climbers can indulge. Its rocks will never draw the international climbing crowd the way that its slopes draw jet-set skiers, but the small crags that sprout by the road to Independence Pass have a special character. The one and two pitch granite routes are frequently of excellent quality, but even nicer is the beauty of the subalpine surroundings. Fall is when the town's name takes on full meaning,when the hills are blanketed not in white powder, but in golden radiance as the trees prepare for winter. Forest Service campgrounds are free and near the cliffs.

CLIMBING

Though a glacier once carved at the Roaring Fork valley, the cliffs near Independence Pass show only occasional evidence of polishing. The granite is typically rough and offers many, albeit often small, handholds; it is also fractured by a number of cracks of all sizes. Some thin, bolt protected slabs appear as well. The cliffs are compact—fifty to 250 feet in height— but they are steep (even overhanging) and often difficult in both a devious and a strenuous sense.

Numerous crags can be found as the road leads from Aspen to Independence Pass, and of these, five have been chosen for this book: Weller Slab, First, Second and Third Grotto Cliffs, and Nude Buttress. Approaches vary from virtually stepping out of the car for the First Grotto Cliff to a half hour uphill scramble for Weller Slab.

ENVIRONMENT

Even though Aspen is famed for its glitter and glamour, summer climbers see little of groomed ski slopes and carpeted condos. Instead, they find an open valley, with hillsides that extend above timberline and refreshing (though sometimes drenching) mountain weather. A road snakes along the valley floor, but so does the turbulent Roaring Fork River, which serves to drown the noise of cars.

As the name implies, the hillsides are resplendent with aspen trees. In the late spring, as the buds break open and the leaves burst forth, the hills transform into pastel green. Because of its 8,000 foot elevation, temperatures remain comfortable throughout the summer—or even turn cold during an afternoon thundershower. But the real magic comes with the onset of fall, when gold is not just trapped in local banks, but also blankets the hillsides, making a broke climber feel rich while sitting on a belay ledge.

Just west of town, the extremely rugged Elk Range offers alpine scenery and climbs. Its most famous peaks, the Maroon Bells, are massive piles of rubble, but cleaner rock is found as well.

Trout fishing in the Roaring Fork and other local streams can be excellent.

While climbing at the Grotto Cliffs, don't forget to check out the origin of the name: across the Roaring Fork, deep chasms have been eroded into the granite valley floor.

Besides its outdoor attractions, Aspen is well known as a cultural center, including a music festival, a ballet, and an art museum. For a listing of what is happening about town, visit the Aspen Activities Center at 623 Hopkins Ave (925-6025).

CLIMBING HISTORY

Aspen has been drawing mountain-oriented people for generations, but not until the late 1950's did any of them deem the scruffy little cliffs worthy of any effort. During the 1960's, a transplanted Colorado Springs climber set up residence and began systematically climbing most of the local cliffs. When he founded *Climbing* magazine, headquartered in Aspen, the region drew even more of the faithful, who would come to visit editors of the magazine. These pilgrims sometimes made an impact on the local routes—freeing problems that had been resisting attempts— but local ski instructors, editors and other resident outdoorfolk have always been the principal movers and shakers of Aspen rock climbing.

CAMPING

A number of campgrounds are found along the road to Independence Pass. Most are free and have no drinking water; of these, Lincoln Gulch may be the nicest. Difficult Campground does have water and charges $5. For further information call the Forest Service at 925-3445, or visit the Ranger Station at the corner of Seventh and Hallam Streets on Highway 82. Showers can be found at the Aspen-Basalt KOA twenty miles northwest of Aspen; they charge $9 per night for two people. Other alternatives include several places for inexpensive dormitory-style lodging: Endeavor Lodge, 905 East Hopkins Ave, 925-2847, $10-$12 per person—this may be the nicest place; Alpina Haus, 935 East Durant, 925-7335, $14; and American Youth Hostel, in the Highlands Inn at base of Aspen Highlands ski lifts, 925-5050, $12 non-members, $9 members. Private baths and color TV's can be had for a bargain at the Inverness Lodge 122 East Durant, 925-8500, $35-$42 per night for a triple room. All quoted prices are the less expensive summer rates. Laudromats are available in town.

SEASONS AND WEATHER

Approximate Months	Typical Temperatures		Likelihood of Precipitation	Frequency of Climbable Days
	High	Low		
Nov-Apr	40's	10's −	high	very low
May-Jun	60's +	30's	medium	high
Jul-Aug	70's +	50's	low-med	very high
Sep-Oct	60's	30's	medium	high

Comments: Afternoon thundershowers are common in summer.

RESTRICTIONS AND WARNINGS

Have fun!

GUIDEBOOKS
A Rock Climber's Guide to Aspen (1985) by Larry Bruce. Available from select shops, including the Ute Mountaineer locally, or from Larry Bruce, 7 Ajax Ave., Aspen, CO 81611.
Aspen Rockclimbing Selected Routes (1979) by Greg Davis. Available from the Ute Mountaineer, 308 South Mill St, Aspen, CO 81611.

GUIDE SERVICES AND EQUIPMENT STORES
The Ute Mountaineer, at 308 South Mill Street, is the headquarters for local information as well as equipment sales. Local guides are available through the Rocky Mountain Climbing School, Dick Jackson, Director, located in the Trolley Car at Rubey Park (corner of Durant and Galena Streets), P.O. Box 2432, Aspen, CO 81612, telephone: 303-925-7625 or 925-7185.

EMERGENCY SERVICES
For help in an emergency, call 911. The Aspen Clinic is at 100 East Main Street, 925-5540; the Aspen Valley Hospital is at 200 Castle Creek Road, 925-1120.

GETTING THERE
Two airlines serve Aspen, as do Trailways buses. Hitch-hiking is also a possibility since considerable traffic crosses Independence Pass. Unfortunately, cars may not be eager to stop on the winding mountain road.

Chester Dreiman on Cryogenics

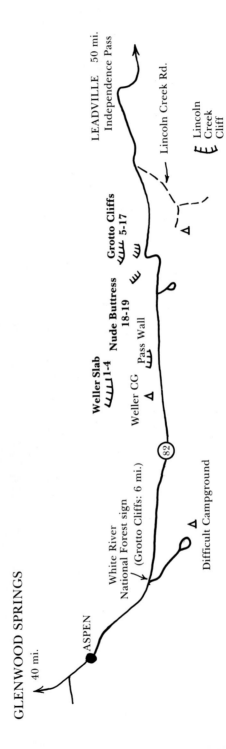

Weller Slab photo: Michael Kennedy
1 **Three Eyed Toad** **5.10+** Lou Dawson and Steve Shea, 1976.
2 **Zanzibar Dihedral** **5.7** Mike Cohen, Steve Kentz and Bruce Shaw, 1970.
3 **Apple Pie** **5.10** Hank Barlow and Steve Kentz, 1971.
4 **Ultra Edge** **5.9** Harvey T. Carter and Tom Merrill, 1970. FFA: Harvey T. Carter, Pete Cleveland and Rozanne Cleveland, 1970.

First Grotto Cliff photo: Michael Kennedy
5 **Twin Cracks** **5.7** Harvey T. Carter and Chuck Vogel, 1968.
6 **Cryogenics** **5.10** Glenn Denny and Bill Forest, early 1960's. FFA 1st pitch:
   John Reppy, about 1968; FFA complete route: Lou Dawson and Michael
   Kennedy, 1974.
7 **Bicentenial** **5.10+** Michael Kennedy and Lou Dawson. FFA: Larry Bruce,
   Lou Dawson and Steve Shea, 1976.
8 **Bicentenial Roof** **5.11+** Henry Barber, 1977.
9 **Pea Brain** **5.12** John Long and Lynn Hill, 1980.
10 **Grotto Wall Traverse** **5.6** **Direct Start and Finish 5.8** Craig Izett and
   David Michaels 1958. FFA: Harvey T. Carter and Annie Carter.

Second and Third Grotto Cliffs

11 Plaque Center 5.10 Lou Dawson and Steve Shea, 1976. Serious runout.

12 Plaque Right 5.9 John Auld, Harvey T. Carter, Rick Gardner and Jake Jacobson.

13 Cohen's Last Problem 5.8 Mike Cohen and Lee Miller, 1967.

14 Tits on a Bull 5.8 Hank Barlow, Lou Dawson and Bob Pimantel 1971.

15 Mind Parasite 5.11 Lou Dawson and Bruce Gordon, 1975. FFA: Lou Dawson and Steve Shea 1976.

16 Necronomicon 5.10 (Climb out left side of cave—hard!) Bruce Kumpf and Steve Shea, 1974.

17 Inner Worlds 5.9 Harvey T. Carter and Chuck Dalebride, 1965.

Nude Buttress photo: Michael Kennedy
18 Blood Bath 5.9 Upper section: Michael Kennedy and Steve Shea, 1973;
lower section: Harvey T. Carter and Lou Dawson, 1973.
19 Brainwashed 5.9 Direct 5.10 Mike Cohen and Lee Miller, 1969. Direct:
Harvey T. Carter, Mike Cohen and Tom Merrill, 1970.

Steve Kentz on Blood Bath photo: Michael Kennedy

Lee Sheftel on Arching Jams, Pericle

PIKE'S PEAK

HIGHLIGHTS

At the edge of a thousand miles of midwestern plains, Pike's Peak rises abruptly 8,000 feet to its 14,410 foot summit. Snaking to the top of this American landmark is a toll road, permitting thousands of tourists to reach the magic 14,000 foot mark, and giving rock climbers easier access to a superb collection of 500 foot granite cliffs. Easier, but not easy. One of the several cirques is appropriately named the Bottomless Pit, and from the 13,000 foot level on the road, one drops down, down, down almost 2,000 feet into the bottom of the cirque where the climbing lies. The pink granite crags reward the effort with a diverse collection of vertical, sweeping cracks. Then comes the walk out.

CLIMBING

Pike's is a massive peak, but it is gentle on all sides. Gentle that is, except for a series of gouges taken out of its eastern flank. In these carved cirques lie a number of granite outcroppings from fifty to 500 feet high. The pink granite is both solid and rough enough for its crystalline teeth to leave marks in one's hands. But though it may not be polished, it is not overly coarse and granular either. Liberally splitting these granite faces are a number of vertical cracks of all sizes. While the climbing follows these cracks fairly religiously, face holds appear as well.

The three cliffs described in this book are perhaps the most visited, but they lie in two different cirques. In the North Pit, morning sun shines on the **Bigger Bagger**, a pinnacle that protrudes from a 500 foot cliff. The most popular route to the summit of the pinnacle involves forty feet of unprotected 5.7 liebacking on the knife edge of the summit block. In the same cirque, Sphinx Rock faces north. Its best climb, **the Flame**, involves three pitches of continuous jamming in a crack that stays cold late into the season. Each of these climbs involve rappel descents. To approach the North Pit, one first parks at about 12,500 feet in elevation, then winds down and into the cirque with a couple miles of moderate walking and scrambling.

Pericle lies at the bottom of the Bottomless Pit. After parking at 13,000 feet, one must drop almost 2,000 feet through fields of huge talus and long scree slopes (interspersed with beautiful alpine meadows) to reach the start of the climb.While the approach may be reasonable, after a full day of climbing (especially for those unaccustomed to the altitude), the hike out can seem endless. Despite these aerobic efforts, the sweeping jam cracks and chimneys on this beautiful cliff are so enticing as to lure even some approach-hating climbers back again. If one is sure enough about the location of the crag's summit, leaving extra equipment there will save having to descend back down to the base of the cliff following a climb and preceeding the long hike up and out.

Another way in would be to hike ten miles up from Manitou Springs. Since cars may not be parked overnight on the Pike's Peak highway, hiking up is the only way to camp overnight near the cliff aside from hitching a ride up the road.

ENVIRONMENT

Pike's Peak stands isolated from other mountains. From the eastern plains, it is easily visible as a remote massif; one can even see the peak from Denver, seventy miles away. At the mountain's feet and at the limit of the midwestern plains, sits the sprawling city of Colorado Springs. From there, Pike's Peak rises 8,000 feet in only ten miles of westward travel. On the peak's back side, the high plateau of the South Platte drainage stretches for miles to the north and west. Numerous crags can be seen dotting its pine forested landscape.

Pike's Peak Highway, the toll road leading to the mountain's summit, is operated by the city of Colorado Springs. Their brochure claims that this is the most famous mountain in the world. This dirt highway is steep—so steep that a policeman checks each car's brake temperature on the descent. Despite the fact that the city charges $4 per person, the road is very popular with summer tourists. As it winds up the mountainside, the road passes lightly forested hillsides up to the tundra that covers the upper section of the mountain. Views from the drive are spectacular; the view from the summit even inspired the song "America the Beautiful."

The hike into North Pit stays at timberline for its length. However, the hike into the Bottomless Pit drops into a valley supporting fifty foot trees. The walk to either cirque offers tremendous views across Colorado Springs and the eastern prairie; on a clear day, it seems that one can see all the way to the Mississippi River. Easily visible at the near edge of Colorado Springs is the red rock of the Garden of the Gods.

While driving through the Springs or climbing at the Garden of the Gods, summer temperatures will be so hot that it may be hard to believe that Pike's Peak could actually be cold. Still, the elevation is great enough that mountain weather can send chilling rains and dense cloud cover to trap the unwary climber.

CLIMBING HISTORY

In 1806 Captain Zebulon Pike, of the United States Army, declared that no man was likely to stand on the summit of "18,581 foot" Pike's Peak. In fact, in 1820 that unlikely event became the first recorded ascent of a 14,000 foot mountain in North America. During the gold rush era of the mid 1800's, "Pike's Peak or Bust" was the slogan for would be gold barons from the east, many of whom would climb to the mountain's summit. Around the turn of the century a commercial toll road was established to relieve people of the strain from the long hike.

Many contemporary rock climbers, keener on adrenalin and pullups than nature walks, welcome a road that saves time in getting to the crags. However, despite the long established climbing community in Colorado Springs and the popularity of hiking or driving Pike's Peak, the granite outcroppings were not climbed until the early 1960's. By then, many of the obvious lines at the Garden of the Gods had been climbed and some climbers became interested in exploring a little further afield. By the late 1960's and early 70's, the South Platte region was opened, and the cliffs on Pike's Peak were extensively developed by topnotch free climbers. Because standards at that time were already high, most of the more aesthetic routes were immediately climbed and by the mid 1970's, the most striking lines had generally been done.

The crags high on Pike's Peak have gradually grown in popularity as climbers continue to search out new haunts. Still, the hearty approach hike is likely to keep the average rock jock at bay for years to come.

CAMPING

Camping near the climbing is not possible unless one hikes the long way in or is dropped off. For those who manage that, the Bottomless Pit offers several beautiful camping possibilities. Otherwise, climbers might be happiest camping near Turkey Rock at the Forest Service campground. In the Colorado Springs area there are numerous private campgrounds, none particularly alluring. The Colorado Springs Youth Hostel, at 17 Farragut Avenue, is another possibility (telephone: 632-5056 or 471-2938). Showers and other facilities can be found in Woodland Park, between Turkey Rock and Pike's Peak, or in Manitou and Colorado Springs.

SEASONS AND WEATHER

Approximate Months	Typical Temperatures High	Low	Likelihood of Precipitation	Frequency of Climbable Days
Oct-May	cold		snow	very low
Jun-Sep	60's+	30's	medium	high

Comments: The North Pit has a slightly shorter season than the Bottomless Pit, and Sphinx Rock is normally not climbed until late July and August. The toll road is not plowed until late spring.

RESTRICTIONS AND WARNINGS

The toll road closes in the evening; ask for the precise time. If one is not out by then, hassles are likely. The road is also expensive ($4 per person) and its steepness demands a strong car.

For the unprepared, mountain weather can throw a chilling wrench into a rock climber's day. Be equipped for cold and thunderstorms.

GUIDEBOOKS

Though various peak-bagger's guidebooks mention the trail to the summit, no public books cover the rock climbing here. One large format picture book does include a few photos of the climbing: "Vertigo Games" (1983) by Glenn Randall. Available from W.R. Publications, 223 Cloverleaf Court, Sioux City, Iowa 51103.

GUIDE SERVICES AND EQUIPMENT STORES

While no guide services are local to the Pike's Peak region, two climbing equipment stores are found in nearby Colorado Springs: Mountain Chalet, 226 North Tejon; and Holubar, 1776 Uintah West.

EMERGENCY SERVICES

In an emergency, contact a patrolman on the Pike's Peak Highway or call 911. The closest hospitals and clinics in Colorado Springs include: Community Health Center, 1301 South 8th, 475-1575; Penrose Hospital, 2215 North Cascade, 630-3300, emergency: 630-3211; St. Francis, East Pike's Peak, 473-6830.

GETTING THERE

Public transportation can be taken to the very summit of Pike's Peak, but this necessitates hiking two miles down the road to start the normal hike into the Pericle cirque (five miles down the road for North Pit). To reach the summit by public transport, use the cog railway from Ruxton Avenue, Manitou Springs. This cog is fairly expensive; another option is to simply walk ten miles up the Barr Trail from the same starting point. To shorten this distance by a couple of miles, use the Mount Manitou Incline Railway to start, also expensive. Manitou Springs can be reached by city bus from Colorado Springs, which can in turn be reached by most major bus and air lines. Hitch hiking up the Pike's Peak Highway is not likely to be very speedy.

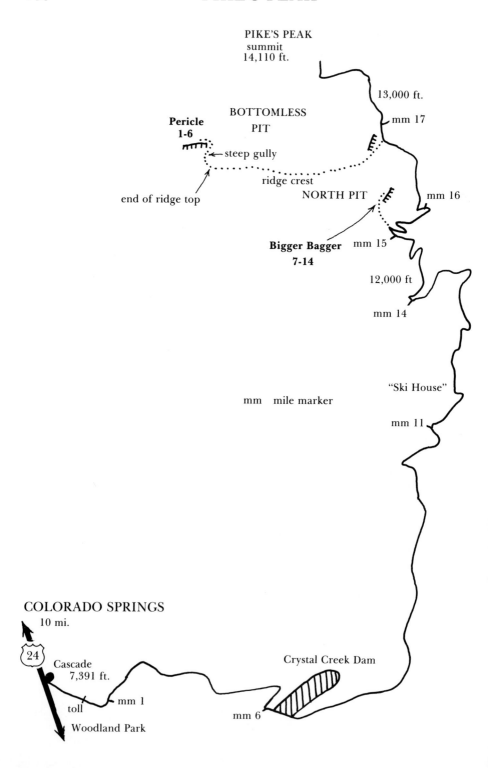

PIKE'S PEAK
summit
14,110 ft.

13,000 ft.

mm 17

BOTTOMLESS
PIT

**Pericle
1-6**

steep gully

ridge crest

end of ridge top

NORTH PIT

mm 16

**Bigger Bagger
7-14**

mm 15

12,000 ft

mm 14

"Ski House"

mm   mile marker

mm 11

COLORADO SPRINGS

10 mi.

24

Cascade
7,391 ft.

Crystal Creek Dam

toll

mm 1

mm 6

Woodland Park

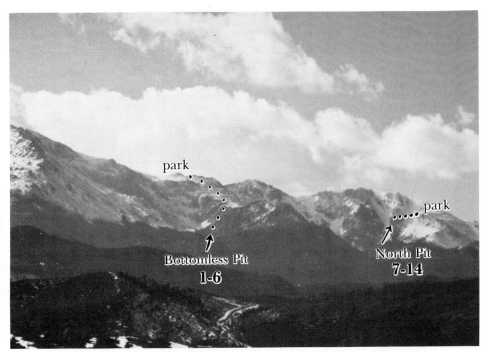

The east flank of Pike's Peak as seen from Colorado Springs

The North Pit as seen from the descent to the Bottomless Pit

Pericle

1 **Free and Easy Chimney II 5.7 or 5.8** (hand crack variation to last pitch) Harvey T Carter and partner, l960's.

2 **Don't Think Twice III 5.9** (hand) Billy Westbay and Cito Kirkpatrick, 1973.

3 **Arching Jams III 5.10 −** (hand) Dan McClure and Billy Westbay, l972.

4 **Pericle Chimney III 5.10 + or 5.11** (ow) Dan McClure, Billy Westbay and Mark Hesse, l972.

5 **Feather Route (originally Empirical) III 5.10 + or 5.11** Harvey T. Carter, l960's, probably not completed. FFA: Dan McClure and Earl Wiggins, l974.

6 **Around the Corner II 5.10** First ascent by two Englishmen. FFA: Billy Westbay and Cito Kirkpatrick, l973.

Bill Nicholson on Finger Fanger

Paul Abrams on the Bigger Bagger pinnacle

Bill Nicholson on Finger Fanger

Sphynx Buttress
7 **The Flame II 5.10** (hands) Dan McClure and Earl Wiggins, 1974.
Bigger Bagger
8 **Normal Route Finish** Use caution on loose block at base of bolt ladder. Don Doucette and Steve Cheyney, late 1960's (with aid via crack).
9 **Finger Fanger III 5.9** (fingers and hands)Steve Cheyney and Peter Croft.
10 **III 5.9+** (large crack) Steve Cheyney and Billy Westbay, 1971.
11 **Gold Wall III 5.10−** (large crack).Use any variation up.
12 **III 5.10−** (undercling and hands). Use any variation up.
13 **Neutron Tide III 5.11c** (hand crack and offwidth through roofs) Leonard Coyne and Peter Mayfield, 1979. Use any variation up.
14 **Solar Wind II 5.11d** (hand crack) Leonard Coyne and Peter Mayfield, 1979.

bolts
5.10 −

8   no pro
5.7

5.10   rappel

5.11d

5.9

5.9+

14

5.8 +

5.11 ow

5.9

5.10

11

10   12   13

9

Gateway Rocks with Pike's Peak in Background

GARDEN OF THE GODS

HIGHLIGHTS
Though Garden of the Gods sandstone turns towards the heavens in spectacular sweeps, many climbers feel that the rock was architected more by the Devil than by Jehova. The crags protrude from the ground like shark fins, with vertically tilted sedimentary beds that feature "dinner plate" holds. These holds can be notoriously loose, but they do produce occasional superb climbs, especially loved by soft rock afficionados. There are perhaps a dozen of these elongated slivers, many between 100 and 350 feet tall. Although nearby camping is available, it is rather urbanized.

CLIMBING
Garden of the Gods sandstone is probably ancient focilized dunes. Strongly crossbedded, then tilted vertically as the Front Range was elevated, they are now free-standing fins of soft rock. Much of the climbing takes place on weathered vertical plates, more or less solidly anchored to the main mass. These plates range in size from tea-cup saucers to flying saucers, and their strength to a large extent determines the desirability of the route; most of the often-climbed popular routes are eventually cleaned up— whether by accident or deliberately. To avoid removing handholds, locals recommend pulling downward—never outward—on the plates.

Because cracks are infrequent and the sandstone can shear next to a nut, most of the protection is in the form of fixed "drilled angle" pitons. The common habit among desert climbers of forcing ½ inch angles into ⅜ inch drilled holes originated at the Garden. With these pitons in place, many climbs need little more than carabiners and slings for protection. Because drilled angles are quite strong, and because standards here have been high since the 1960's, runouts are frequently long—which can be especially unnerving on steep balance moves on loose holds. There are, however, also a few excellent crack climbs, sometimes on extremely solid rock that defies the Garden's reputation.

The Park is in danger of being closed to climbing due to the smear marks left by climbing-shoe rubber, chalk marks, and other unsightly blemishes. Please read and heed the *RESTRICTIONS AND WARNINGS* section to help minimize tensions with the park management.

ENVIRONMENT

As the sun sets over nearby 14,410 foot Pike's Peak, the red sandstone at the Garden of the Gods almost glows in the desert landscape. Until the 1880's, the Garden was a worshipping ground for Ute Indians who wintered in the area. They were driven to reservations in Utah by encroaching white settlers. Plans by the settlers included carving Gateway Rock into giant figures; instead, the Park was ceded by its private owners to the city of Colorado Springs in 1907.

The Garden is a melting pot of ecosystems: the Great Plains grasslands meet the mountain forest and Southwestern pinyon-juniper woodlands. The beauty of this landscape, especially as the sun drops low in the sky and summer temperatures moderate, belies the fact that the Garden is a city park. However, the throngs of tourists and the lack of quality camping nearby remind one that this is no wilderness climbing area; in fact, the Park even closes after dark. Urban Colorado Springs begins just outside Park boundaries.

CLIMBING HISTORY

Climbing at the Garden of the Gods began almost as early as roped fifth class climbing was initiated in the United States. Some of Colorado's earliest technical pioneers played at the Garden, climbing several ridges and chimneys on these sandstone fins during the 1920's and 30's. During the 1940's, home-made pitons allowed the establishment of climbs as hard as 5.8, but it was in the 1950's that a revolution in protection was invented. The nearby Fort Carson Army station produced many soft steel angle pitons. Sawed off to three inches in length and hammered into drilled holes, this protection system provided good security, even on long runouts.

During the 1960's a few radically overhanging aid routes were ascended using "drilled angles," but the usual trend was to use them sparcely as protection on free routes. From the 1960's to the early 1980's, Colorado Springs residents (including local college students) climbed many lines of extreme difficulty.

CAMPING

Tent camping in the Colorado Springs area is grim for climbers with a sense of aesthetics. Nearby campgrounds tend to be oriented towards those with Recreational Vehicles. This situation will, more than anything, keep the Garden more of a quick stop-over climbing area than a place to hang out for a week or longer. A nearby camping area is Pike's Peak Campground, 320 Manitou Avenue, Manitou Springs, 685-9459. (This campground is next to the city swimming pool and the trail leading up Pike's Peak.) Another is the Crystal Kangaroo Campground on Crystal Park Road, 685-5010. Campgrounds may require reservations in the summer; they cost $8-$11 per site. About seventeen miles northwest of Colorado Springs (five miles north of Woodland Park) are a number of Forest Service campgrounds that are in the $4-$5 range, but do not include showers. Also available is the Colorado Springs Youth Hostel, 17 North Farragut Avenue, 471-2938 or 632-5056; rates start at $6.

SEASONS AND WEATHER

Approximate Months	Typical Temperatures High	Low	Likelihood of Precipitation	Frequency of Climbable Days
Nov-Mar	40's+	20's	med-low	med-high
Apr-May	60's+	30's+	med-low	very high
Jun-Aug	80's+	50's	medium	high
Sep-Oct	70's−	40's−	low	very high

Comments: Summer rain is likely to come in the form of passing thundershowers.

RESTRICTIONS AND WARNINGS

To reduce the likelihood of the city closing the Park to climbing (a real possibility), local climbers have established self-imposed rules banning the use of chalk, and of leaving only rust-colored slings at rappel anchors. Bouldering is also disapproved of because of the rubber and chalk marks usually left behind. Some climbers have begun cleaning boulders to placate Park administrators. The city also bans solo climbing; penalized by up to a $300 fine and 90 days in jail. It is illegal to climb or descend the Tourist Gulley on North Gateway Rock because it encourages incompetents to scramble up the gully. The Park closes in the evening. Take care on the loose flakes; if possible, do not pull outward on them.

GUIDEBOOKS

Soft Touch (1983) by Mark Rolofson. Available in many Colorado mountaineering stores or from Mark Rolofson, PO Box 732, Boulder, CO 80306.

GUIDE SERVICES AND EQUIPMENT STORES

Equipment shops in Colorado Springs include Holubar, at 1776 Uintah West, and Mountain Chalet, 226 North Tejon.

EMERGENCY SERVICES

In case of emergency, contact the ranger at Park headquarters or call 911. Hospitals in Colorado Springs include: Community Health Center, 1301 South 8th, 475-1575; Penrose Hospital, 2215 North Cascade, 630-3300, emergency: 630-3211; St. Francis, East Pike's Peak, 473-6830.

GETTING THERE

All major forms of public transportation are available to Colorado Springs. From downtown, city bus service will take one to Garden Drive, from which two miles of walking leads to the climbing area.

North Ridge of Montezuma

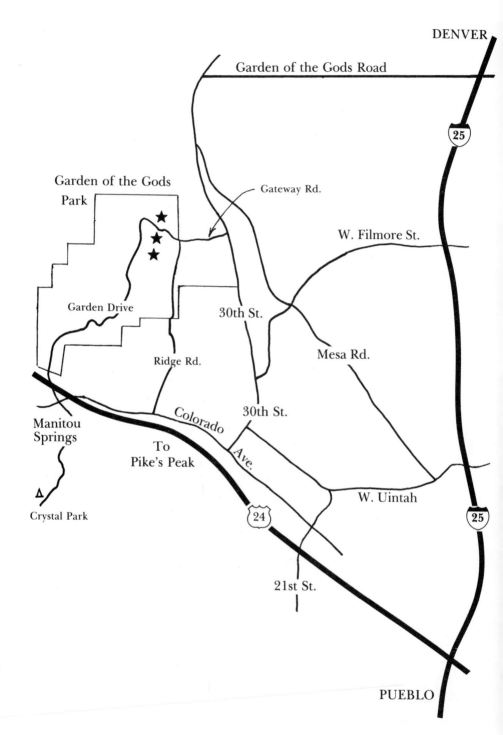

Dale Goddard on Amazing Grace

Tower of Babel

North Gateway Rock

Descent: It is common to rappel after the first pitches. From the summit, most people scramble to and down Tourist Gully, though descending it is illegal. Legally, it is best to descend ledges diagonalling south on the east side; unfortunately, these ledges are not as safe and frequently become icy in winter.

1 **Anaconda 5.11** Layton Kor and Gary Zeigler. FFA: Earl Wiggins, Jim Dunn and John Sherwood, 1975. Pure crack climbing. Bypass the 1st potential hanging belay. Nuts to 3½ in. Rappel 75 ft east, then descend East Ledges.

2 **Borgoff's Blunder 5.10** Michael Borgoff, mid 1960's. Complete FFA: Pete Croff and Herby Hendricks. Fixed pro except long runners for pothole threads; optional large nuts.

3 **Rainbow Bridge 5.10 +** Ed Webster and Peter Mayfield, 1979.

4 **Over the Rainbow 5.10** 1st pitch: Leonard Coyne and Ed Webster, 1978; complete: Ed Webster and Brian Becker, 1978. Fixed pro; wire or thin sling needed to thread bolt. Loose rock.

North Gateway Rock

5 Pot of Gold 5.8 Ed Webster and Peter Mayfield, 1976.

6 Henry the Pig 5.8 Leonard Coyne, Ed Bailey and Mark Rolofson, 1976.

7 Pete and Bob's Crack 5.9 FFA: Steve Cheyney. Nuts to 3 in. #10 hex in pothole protects start.

8 Link-Up 5.9 Bring slings and large nuts.

9 Pete and Bob's 5.11 Pete Croff and Bob Stauch, mid 1960's. FFA 2nd pitch: Bill Mummery and Mike Grey, 1968; complete: Kurt Rasmussen, 1973.

10 Fastest Drill (in the West) 5.8 Ed Webster, Mack Johnson and Dave Sweet, 1978. Medium nuts for climb and upper belay.

11 Trigger Finger 5.10 Dirk Taylor and Dave Hodges, 1979.

12 Cowboy Boot Crack 5.7 Medium nuts. Poor pro on upper route.

South Gateway Rock

13 Staircase 5.7 (first pitch) Steve Cheyney, Pete Croff and Bob Stauch. Medium nuts.

✓**14 Practice Slab 5.1-5.8** Stanley Boucher and Vernon Twombly, 1945. Ascend chopped steps on right to set up top-rope from iron bar.

✓**15 West Point Crack 5.7** U.S. Army, 1961. FFA: Harvey T. Carter. Fixed pro; nuts optional.

16 Credibility Gap 5.9 Gary Zeigler and John Auld, mid 1960's. FFA: Morgan Gadd and Skip Hamilton. Excellent fixed pro; bring 1½ in. and 3½ in. nuts.

Kindergarten Rock and Montezuma Tower

17 North Ridge of Kindergarten Rock 5.4 Bob Ormes, 1925. Climb gully just east of N. Ridge, then short wall to gain ridge.

✓**18 North Ridge of Montezuma Tower 5.7/5.8** U.S. Army, 1945. FFA: Harvey T. Carter, about 1950. Fixed pro except sling for pothole thread; nuts optional. Two ropes for rappel.

Kindergarten Rock with Montezuma Tower

Fred Aschert on Pete and Bob's

Turkey Rocks

TURKEY ROCKS

HIGHLIGHTS

The headwaters of the South Platte River flow through classic western terrain: rolling, pine-forested hills, with white water streams. Scattered through almost a thousand square miles of hills are numerous rough granite crags that hold face climbs and many of Colorado's finest crack routes. Of these many crags, the Turkey Rock complex is the most popular because of its incredible concentration of routes, and because it is adjacent to a drive-in Forest Service campground. These rocks certainly offer some of Colorado's finest crag climbing.

CLIMBING

The Turkey Rock area consists of two adjacent cliffs: Turkey Rock and Turkey Tail. Turkey Rock holds several 5.7-5.9 crack routes that are almost 350 feet long. Turkey Tail, in contrast, has few routes less than 5.10 in difficulty. The rock is about 250 feet high, and its vertical walls are littered with overhangs—and cracks that split them. Both cliffs are pinkish granite that are at once solid and rough. While there is no glacial polish, neither is there the coarse crumbliness of some desert granite. Descents from each rock involve a 3rd class scramble down the back side.

Because the rocks face southeast, climbing is often possible year-round despite the 8,000 foot elevation. Still, winter snow can obstruct the last two miles of never-plowed dirt roads.

Many climbers will wonder why the famous Cynical Pinnacle was omitted from this book. It was not included because the rock is closed during most of the climbing season due to peregrine falcon nesting.

ENVIRONMENT

Open pine forests that are a pleasure to hike in and clear, trout-bearing creeks rushing through gentle valleys—these are the scenes that draw outdoorsmen to Colorado from around the country. The high peaks are off in the distance, usually invisible, but the elevation of the plateau forming the South Platte watershed keeps the fresh atmosphere of the mountains. Though mid-summer mid-day can be uncomfortably hot, cool mornings inspire one to activity. If one wants to escape from other climbers, the massive watershed of the South Platte is littered with granite outcroppings, many of which are rarely touched.

CLIMBING HISTORY

Climbing in the South Platte was explored by Colorado Springs residents in the early 1970's. Though the sandstone crags of the Garden of the Gods were at their doorstep, climbers from the Springs knew that the nearby Pike's Peak massif and environs must hold some granite outcroppings. Within an hour's drive from the city, they found the Turkey Rock complex; further north, the remainder of the South Platte drainage awaited exploration.

While Boulder and Denver climbers played a considerable role in developing the northern parts of the South Platte, Turkey Rock was kept quiet by the Springs climbers. They knew that they had a treasure here, and they were also quite capable of doing the hardest climbs themselves. By the 1980's, however, an increasing number of non-Colorado Springs climbers were visiting the area, including well travelled foreigners. The publication of an article on the area in 1983 and guidebooks in 1984 spurred further recognition for what is undoubtably one of Colorado's finest collections of crack routes.

CAMPING

A free Forest Service campground is within walking distance of the cliffs. It features toilets and drinking water. The nearest laundry facilities and grocery stores are in Woodland Park, fifteen miles south.

SEASONS AND WEATHER

Approximate Months	Typical Temperatures High	Low	Likelihood of Precipitation	Frequency of Climbable Days
Nov-Mar	40's −	10's +	medium	medium
Apr-May	60's +	30's +	med-high	high
Jun-Aug	80's	50's	medium	high
Sep-Oct	60's	30's	low	very high

Comments: Brief afternoon thundershowers are common in the summer. The final two miles of dirt road may be impassable in the winter, due to snow.

RESTRICTIONS AND WARNINGS

Though Turkey Rock and Turkey Tail are on National Forest Service land, walking the shortest distance from the campground to the cliffs involves crossing private land owned by the Turkey Rock Estates. They DO NOT want anyone trespassing, and have been known to call the sheriff and/or shoot at offending climbers. Instead, follow the dirt road around to the back side of the cliffs where there is legal Forest Service access.

GUIDEBOOKS

For Turkey's Only (1984) by Steve Cheyney. Covers the Turkey Rocks and nearby Sheepsnose, as well as the South Platte's largest cliff: Big Rock Candy Mountain. Available in many Colorado stores or from Steve Cheyney, 309 Elmwood, Colorado Springs, CO 80907.
The Hard Stuff (1984) by Mark Rolofson. Covers Cynical Pinnacle and

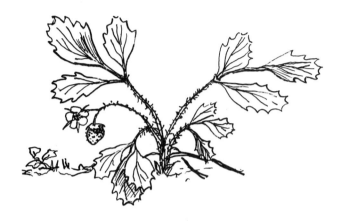

miscellaneous other crags in addition to the Turkey Rock area. Available in many Colorado stores or from Mark Rolofson, PO Box 732, Boulder CO 80306.

The Brown Book of Lies (1983) by Peter Hubbel. Covers more of the South Platte region than the other books, but does not include the Turkey Rock area. Available in many Colorado stores or from Vertical Adventures Inc., 1580 Taft, Lakewood CO 80215.

GUIDE SERVICES AND EQUIPMENT STORES

The nearest equipment stores are in Colorado Springs, forty miles away. They include: Holubar, 1776 Uintah West, and Mountain Chalet, 226 North Tejon.

EMERGENCY SERVICES

In case of emergency, contact the Jefferson County Sheriff by telephoning the operator and asking for "Enterprise 0211." The nearest hospitals are in Colorado Springs, 40 miles away. Community Health Center, 1301 S. 8th, 475-1575; Penrose Hospital, 2215 North Cascade, 630-3300, emergency: 630-3211; Saint Francis, East Pike's Peak, 473-6830.

GETTING THERE

No public transportation serves the South Platte region. Hitch hiking from Colorado Springs or Denver is possible, but is likely to be slow.

Hidetaka Suzuki on Rasmussen's Crack

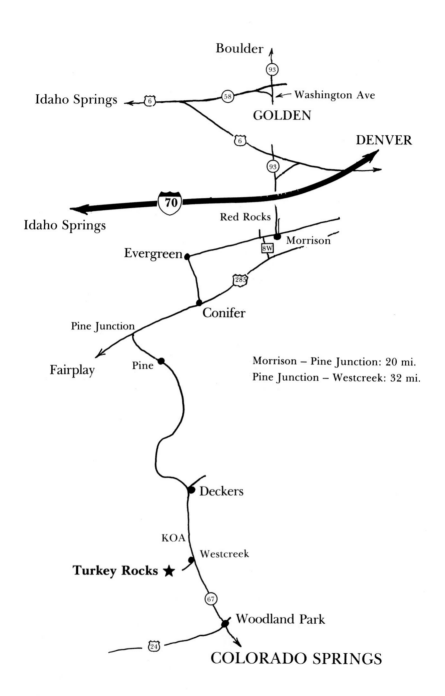

Boulder

93

Idaho Springs ← 6   58   ← Washington Ave

GOLDEN

6

DENVER

93

70

Idaho Springs   Red Rocks

8W   Morrison

Evergreen

285

Conifer

Pine Junction

Fairplay   Pine

Morrison – Pine Junction: 20 mi.
Pine Junction – Westcreek: 32 mi.

Deckers

KOA

Westcreek

Turkey Rocks ★

67

Woodland Park

24

COLORADO SPRINGS

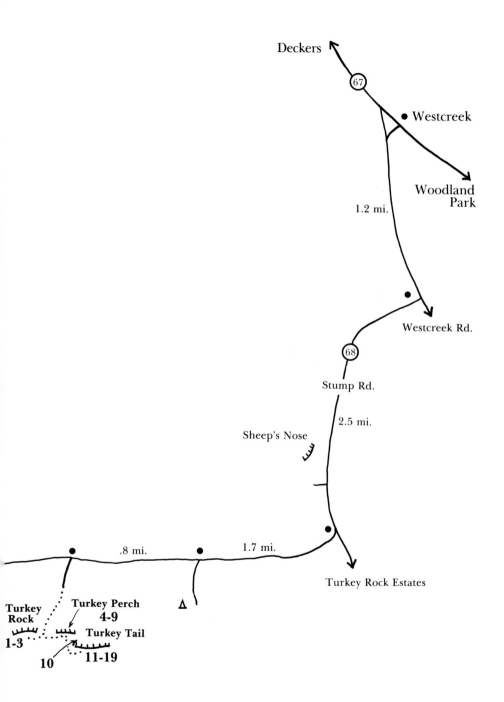

Turkey Rocks

Whimsical Dreams photo: Charlie Fowler

Turkey Rock
  1 **Gobbler's Grunt 5.9−** Skip Hamilton and Steve Cheyney, early 1970's.
  2 **Turkey Shoot 5.9−** John Sherwood and Gary Garreit, 1975.
  3 **Satyr's Asshole 5.10** The last pitch has a runout on loose, 5.10− flakes.

Turkey Perch
  4 Reefer Madness 5.9
  5 Ragger Bagger 5.9
  6 Gobble Up 5.9 The crack eats belay ropes if climbed in 2 pitches.
  7 Disappearing Act 5.9
  8 5.7
  9 Left Handed Jew 5.7
10 Quivering Quill 5.10 FFA: Jim Dunn and Earl Wiggens, about 1974.

Gobble Up

Turkey Tail

11 Piece of Cake 5.11 Jim Dunn and Ajax Greene, 1972.

12 Rasmussen's Crack 5.10 Kurt Rasmussen, early 1970's.

13 Snively's Crack 5.8 or 5.9(with direct finish)Doug Snively, early 1970's.

14 Whimsical Dreams 5.11 Jim Dunn and Brian Teale, 1975.

15 For Turkeys Only 5.11+ Jim Dunn and Bryan Becker, 1976. Bring tube chocks.

16 Drumstick Direct 5.10+ FFA: Doug Snively and Dan McClure.
17 Turkey's Turd 5.11 (or 5.8 first pitch) Jim Dunn and John Hall, 1975.
18 Journey to Ixtlan 5.12− Leonard Coyne and Peter Mayfield, 1978.
19 Beauty and the Beast 5.12+ John Allen, 1981.

Redgarden Wall

BOULDER

HIGHLIGHTS

Three major climbing areas lie within five minutes' drive from downtown Boulder, Colorado: Eldorado Canyon, the Flatirons, and Boulder Canyon. A city of over 70,000 people in size, Boulder sits where the Rocky Mountains abruptly rise out of the Midwestern plains. The climbing is on the walls of canyons that pierce the foothills, and on pinnacles that jut from those hills. The cliffs hold one to eight pitch routes on solid sandstone and granite. The major drawback for the climber visiting the Boulder region is a dirth of quality camping.

CLIMBING

Boulder climbing is not only accessible, it is also excellent and diverse. Six miles south of Boulder, Eldorado Canyon offers by far the most famous and popular climbing in the region. Its metamorphosed sandstone is extremely solid and has a delightful silky texture. Though cracks are frequently encountered, Eldorado is noted for its face climbing on small edges with intricate combination moves. The crags that make up this canyon vary considerably in size, with most climbs at least two pitches in length. Many routes are six short pitches—eight in the extreme. Steepness is almost the rule in Eldorado, with a number of routes close to vertical. Approaches range from five to fifteen minutes along good trails, and descents from almost all routes can be made on foot, though extreme caution must be exercised on the 3rd class slabs.

Along the six mile stretch from downtown Boulder to Eldorado

Canyon are the most visible crags of the Boulder area. The Flatirons are a vast maze of rocks that are a softer, less metamorphosed sandstone than Eldorado. The cliffs generally lean uphill and are low angle on the major exposed face, steep and shorter on the other faces. Some of these exposed low angle slabs are a 1,000 feet long. Among the Flatirons described in this book is the largest, the 3rd Flatiron, and one of the most spectacular, the Maiden. The Maiden is somewhat exceptional in that it is a thin fin of a rock that projects to a summit. The overhanging rappel off the Maiden's summit is one of the most spectacular descents most climbers will ever do. Approaches to these Flatirons rarely involve more than an hour of hiking (including some hefty uphill).

The third climbing attraction is the numerous granite crags scattered along Boulder Canyon. The canyon begins at the edge of town, and its first crag, the Dome, is only a mile up the road. Ten miles further—and just before the canyon opens back up—is Castle Rock, the most famous of Boulder's granite cliffs. Though some face climbing is encountered, most of the routes follow excellent deep cracks on the steep 250 foot face. The approach involves little more than getting out of the car.

A fourth very popular area is the superb bouldering on Flagstaff Mountain, just five minutes by car from Boulder and overlooking the city. Evenings after work and school find a great number of climbers here. It is a magical place to watch the sun go down and the lights of Boulder come out.

ENVIRONMENT

The Midwestern plains stretch eastward a thousand miles from Boulder to the Mississippi River. But at Boulder's western edge, a massive fault pushes foothills abruptly upward. Though the hills jutting up behind town only rise about 3,000 feet from Boulder's 5,400 foot elevation, they obscure views of nearby taller mountains, including 14,255 foot Long's Peak.

The plains east of Boulder are covered in a patchwork of urban sprawl, ranch land, and prairie. But where the hills begin, so does an open, coniferous forest.

Eldorado is a tight little canyon rimmed with vertical sandstone walls and cut by a roaring stream. The sandstone is a colorful blend of red and orange, with streaks of bright yellow lichens painted over sections of cliff. Noise from the river helps to drown out conversations. This would make the place feel less crowded than it normally is, except that it forces people to shout between belay station and climber. Often one can hear the party across the river far better than one's own partner.

One drawback to Eldorado is the frequent crowds, especially on a spring or fall weekend. In the mid-summer, because of the heat, climbing is impractical except on shady walls or at the beginning or end of the day. Evenings after work are often busy with climbers rushing to do short routes on the Bastille or other convenient cliff.

While many of the Flatirons are rarely touched by climbers and can offer a remarkably remote experience, the Maiden and the Third Flatiron can see heavy traffic. Expect at least the possibility of encountering other climbers, especially on a weekend. Early in the morning and in the spring, the hour long approach hikes are delightful: flowers bloom, dew sparkles, deer graze. The Flatirons are in the Boulder Mountain Park System, likely one of the most beautiful and extensive city parks in the world.

Boulder Canyon suffers from having a busy road parallel to the rushing stream its entire length. This road does make the climbing convenient, and at Castle Rock at least, most of the climbing is out of sight of the highway.

Colorado is a land of sunshine, and the cliffs get their full share of it. Even in mid-winter, south facing rocks can offer excellent climbing.

CLIMBING HISTORY

As early as the 1920's, a few radicals were climbing the Flatirons. "Radical" because at that time no one else was concerned with anything "less" than a mountain. But though these ventures into rock climbing happened earlier than elsewhere in the country, little development in standards or interest occured until the end of the 1940's. Then a few aid climbs appeared on the Flatirons that involved the first ascents of major overhangs and the first placement of bolts in the region.

Though steep, these Flatiron climbs were only two or three pitches in length. Eldorado's longer climbs were excessively intimidating until the **Redguard** route was established in 1956. The first ascentionists assumed that it would require aid, but it surprised them by going entirely free at 5.7. This climb coincided with the beginning of a new era in Boulder area climbing. Within the next few years, numerous climbs were established throughout the Boulder region, but especially in Eldorado. In reaction to a competitive joke, the first 5.10 was climbed in 1959, though it was many years ahead of its time.

During the early 1960's, climbing in Eldorado exploded with an energetic rush of new routes. **The Naked Edge** was climbed as an A4 route, but free climbing at the 5.9 standard was common on mixed routes. The important issue was speed, free and aid being mixed as necessary to climb the wall quickly; after all, crags were still viewed more as training grounds for mountains than as interesting in their own right.

In the mid and late 1960's, free climbing on crags became an end in itself. Visiting Californians were the initial inspiration, but a few locals quickly became interested in extreme difficulties of moves, whether on boulders or on roped climbs. After top-rope practice, **Supremacy Crack** was led in 1966, becoming one of the first 5.11's in the country. As the 1960's progressed into the 1970's, free climbing took on increasing significance, so that by the end of the decade, few aid climbs remained unfreed.

The 1971 free ascent of the **Naked Edge** (5.11) was a milestone in this movement; the route has now become one of the classic free climbs in North America. Indeed, during the 1970's the density of superb climbs in Eldorado put the Canyon on the map as one of the three leading centers of rock climbing in North America—along with Yosemite and the Shawangunks. Because so much good climbing is concentrated so close to a city, Boulder has become a haven for displaced climbers from around the world. Many of the current hardest climbs are being established by resident foreign climbers.

CAMPING

Camping is Boulder's biggest downfall. The only camping in Eldorado Canyon is available from The International Alpine School, located north of the swimming pool ($8 per site). There is a typically sterile and expensive ($9) KOA at 5856 Valmont on the eastern outskirts of town (the climbing is all on the western side of town, with no public transportation between). The KOA does have showers available and the fee is for two people. The only other sanctioned camping is twenty-five miles into the hills west of Boulder. Kelly Dahl campground charges $5 after Memorial Day (approximately May 30) and has water available (three miles south of Nederland on Hwy 119). Rainbow Lakes, somewhat further away, is free, but somewhat further (six and one half miles north of Nederland on Hwy 72, then five miles west on Arapahoe Glacier Road). For more information on the camping areas, visit the Forest Service Station at 2995 Baseline, Room 16, or call 444-6001.

Perhaps better than camping out is the Boulder International Youth Hostel. It is $6 for members, $8 for non-members—which is far cheaper than Boulder's motels (which start at about $30). The hostel is located at 1107 12th St. on "the Hill," telephone: 442-9304. The Nederland Youth Hostel is only $4.50, but is located 20 miles from town up Boulder Canyon. It is fairly close to Boulder Canyon's Castle Rock, and could easily be reached by hitch-hiking from there. (1005 Jackson St, Nederland, telephone: 258-9925.)

SEASONS AND WEATHER

Approximate Months	Typical Temperatures		Likelihood of Precipitation	Frequency of Climbable Days
	High	Low		
Nov-Mar	40's	20's	med-low	low-med
Apr-May	60's	30's+	med	high-med
Jun-Aug	80's	50's	low-med	high
Sept-Oct	60's	30's	low	very high

Comments: Afternoon thundershowers are common in the summer.

RESTRICTIONS AND WARNINGS

Eldorado is a State Park and charges $1 per person or $2 per carload (all you can fit) to enter. For extended visits, an annual pass ($20) pays off for those with a car.

GUIDEBOOKS

Rocky Heights, A Guide to Boulder Free Climbs 1980 by Jim Erickson. Currently out of print, but available locally from many climbing equipment stores and several bookstores. One of the finest guidebooks written, Erickson's witty route descriptions are often as fun as the climbing itself.

Boulder Climbs, A Pictorial Guide to Boulder Climbs (1985) by Richard Rossiter. Available locally from any climbing store or from Richard Rossiter, PO Box 3004, Eldorado Springs, CO 80025. Popular, no language barrier, and more comprehensive than Erickson's book.

High Over Boulder (1985) by Pat Ament. Available locally from several climbing stores, including Neptune Mountaineering, 627 South Broadway, Boulder, CO 80303. This is the latest comprehensive compiling of Boulder area routes.

GUIDE SERVICES AND EQUIPMENT STORES

Boulder is saturated with technical mountaineering equipment stores, most located along Broadway and conveniently reached. The Yellow Pages of the phone book will locate them all. A number of guide services also serve the local climbs. The International Alpine School / Boulder Mountain Guides is located north of the swimming pool at the mouth of Eldorado Canyon: Eldorado Springs, CO 80025, telephone: 303-494-4904. Operating out of Denver are the Forrest Climbing School: 1136 Speer Boulevard, Denver, CO 80204, telephone: 303-433-3373; and the Eastern Mountain Sports Climbing School, 1428 15th St, Denver, CO 80202, telephone: 303-571-1160. There are also numerous private guides and smaller guide services operating in the Boulder area whose flyers one can pick up in the climbing stores.

EMERGENCY SERVICES

Several hospitals exist in Boulder, including: Boulder Memorial Hospital at 311 Mapleton Avenue, telephone: 443-0230 or 441-0447; and the Boulder Community Hospital at 1100 Balsam, telephone: 440-2273 or 440-2037. Boulder is also a haven for numerous "alternative" health care facilities; they can be found in the Yellow Pages. For emergencies in Eldorado Canyon, first try to locate a ranger in the toll-booth. Otherwise, call the Boulder County Sheriff at 911 emergency, 441-3370 non-emergency.

GETTING THERE

All the major avenues of public transportation (international airport, train, bus) serve Denver, thirty miles south of Denver. The RTD bus runs from Denver to Boulder many times per day. No public transportation serves Eldorado Canyon itself, but hitch-hiking is common.

Bastille Crack, 2nd pitch

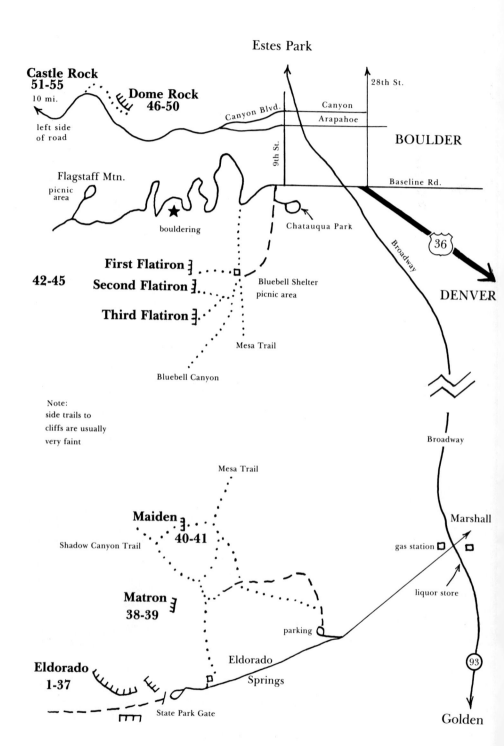

Wind Tower

1 **Wind Ridge II 5.6** Layton Kor and Jane Culp, 1959.

2 **Tagger II 5.10** Larry Dalke and Pat Ament, 1962. FFA: Jim Erickson and Jim Walsh, 1968.

3 **Calypso II 5.6** Layton Kor, Larry Dalke and Pat Ament, 1961.

The Bastille

Jim Evans on the Bastille Crack

The Bastille

4 Werk Supp II 5.9 Pat Ament and Ralph Warsfield, 1964. FFA: Dave Rearick and Pat Ament, 1964.

5 Bastille Crack III 5.7 FA: Army climbers early 1950's. FFA: Layton Kor and Stan Shepard, 1959. This fine climb is perhaps the most popular route in Eldorado. Northcutt Variation (left start) 5.10+ Ray Northcutt, 1959.

6 Outer Space II 5.10− Layton Kor and Steve Komito, 1961. FFA: Jim Erickson, Pat Ament and Diana Hunter, 1971.

 7 Wide Country III 5.11 Roger Briggs and Leo Foster, 1967. FFA: (Jim Erickson first pitch) Duncan Ferguson and Don Peterson, 1972.

 8 X-M III 5.10− Pat Ament and Layton Kor, 1962. FFA: Larry Dalke and Terry O'Donnell, 1967. Nasty runout on second (crux) pitch without small to medium brass nuts.

 9 The Northwest Corner III 5.10+ Layton Kor and Peter Lev, 1959. FFA: Pat Ament, 1966.

10 West Buttress III 5.9 Layton Kor and Carl Pfiffner, 1959. FFA: Layton Kor and Larry Dalke, 1964.

Roger Whitehead on the West Buttress

South Buttress Redgarden Wall

11 **C'Est La Vie II 5.11** Pat Ament and Jeff Wheeler, 1962. FFA: Dave Ohlson and Bob Williams, 1973.

12 **Genesis II 5.10+ or 5.12+** Jack Turner and Bob Culp, 1962 (A5). FFA: 5.10+ to bolts (popular): John Bragg, 1974. Complete FFA: Jim Collins, 1979 (runout).

13 **Anthill Direct III 5.8+ or 5.9−** Layton Kor and Rick Tidrick, 1961. Touch 'n Go is the best start. One of the best 5.8 routes in Eldorado.

Redgarden Wall – South Buttress

Redgarden Wall

14 Redguard Route III 5.7 Dick Bird, Chuck Merley, Dallas Jackson, Dale Johnson and Cary Huston, 1956. The first route on the Redgarden Wall. Variation to the Lower Meadow, 5.6; Dale Johnson and partners, 1956.

15 Touch 'n' Go II 5.8 Pat Ament and Gary Spitzer, 1966.

16 T-2 IV 5.10 Layton Kor and Gerry Roach, 1959. FFA: Dave Rearick and Bob Culp, 1962. One of the most popular routes in Eldorado.

17 Jules Verne IV 5.11 Larry Dalke and Pat Ament, 1967. FFA complete route: Steve Wunsch and Jim Erickson, 1975. Serious runout on fourth (5.11−) pitch.

18 Kloeberdanz III 5.11− Layton Kor and Larry Dalke, 1963. FFA: Steve Wunsch and Jim Erickson, 1974. Many parties only climb the first pitch roof (crux).

19 Guenese II 5.11 Layton Kor and Ron Foreman, 1962. FFA: Steve Wunsch, Scott Stewart and Jim Erickson, 1972. First pitch runout.

20 Rosy Crucifixion II 5.10− Layton Kor and Jack Turner, 1962. FFA complete route: Jim Erickson, Ed Wright and Steve Wood, 1970.

21 Ruper II 5.8 Layton Kor and Ed Risley, 1961.

22 Grand Giraffe II 5.9 Layton Kor and George Hurley, 1960. Bring large nuts to 4 inches.

23 Superslab III 5.10+ Layton Kor and Rick Horn, 1961. FFA: Richard Smith, Pat Ament and Tom Ruwitch, 1967.

24 The Naked Edge IV 5.11 Layton Kor, Bob Culp and Rick Horn 1962 and 1964. FFA complete route: Jim Erickson and Duncan Ferguson, 1971.

25 Upper Ruper II 5.8 Layton Kor and Bob Culp, 1961. First pitch slightly runout.

26 Alice in Bucketland II 5.8+ Scott Woodruff and Dan Hare, 1976.

27 Upper Grand Giraffe II 5.6 Layton Kor and George Hurley, 1960. Long runouts.

Rosy Crucifixion

Lower Redgarden Wall

Left side, Lower Redgarden Wall

Upper Redgarden Wall

Leonard Coyne on Guenese

West Face Redgarden Wall

West Face Redgarden Wall

28 Mellow Spur III 5.11+ Larry Dalke and Roger Dalke, 1967. FFA: John Bragg and Steve Wunsch, 1975.

29 Vertigo III 5.11− Dave Dornan and Peter Lev, 1961. FFA: Pat Ament and Roger Briggs 1966. FFA direct finish: Henry Barber and John Stannard, 1973.

30 Yellow Spur III 5.9 or 5.10− direct finish Layton Kor and Dave Dornan, 1959. FFA: Royal Robbins and Pat Ament, 1964. One of the best and most popular routes in Eldorado.

31 Swanson's Arete III 5.5 Stan Shepard and partners, 1960.

32 The Great Zot III 5.7 Bob Culp and Stan Shepard, 1960.

33 Rewritten III 5.7 George Hurley, Bob Culp and John Link, 1967.

34 Green Spur III 5.9 Dallas Jackson and Dave Dornan, 1964. FFA: Larry Dalke, 1964.

35 Grandmother's Challenge II 5.10. Layton Kor, Pat Ament and Dean Moore 1963. FFA: Jim Erickson and John Behrens 1968.

36 Darkness Til Dawn II 5.9+ Jeff Sherman, John Ruger and Hunter Smith, 1974.

37 Green Slab Direct III 5.9 Bob Culp and Henry Huermann, 1961.

The Matron

√ **38 East Face II 5.5** Karl Gustavson and Skip Green, 1951. Start 300 feet uphill after climbing a short chimney to a large block. Climb 20 feet up one of two parallel cracks (left is 5.6), then right to a roof, belay at the tree above. Continue up to East Ridge.

s √**39 East Ridge II 5.5** Bill Eubanks and Brad VanDiver and Stan Black, 1948. Start 30 feet uphill, angle left with 5.5 climbing to tree on ridge.

The Maiden

40 North Face III 5.6 Roy Peak and Mark Taggart, 1944. Slightly runout. Two pitches are not shown: 1) downclimb and traverse left (5.6 poor pro), belay at tree. 2) Angle up left 40 feet then down to belay (5.5)—Walton Traverse variation.

41 East Ridge III 5.10 or 5.7 C1 Dale Johnson, Phil Robertson and Cary Huston, 1953. FFA: Steve Wunsch and Diana Hunter, 1970. A 5.5 start begins right of 5.10 start.

Flatirons

ᔕ✓ **42 Third Flatiron East Face III 5.3** Earl and Floyd Millard, 1906. Runout, but the most classic route in the Boulder area.

43 Second Flatiron Southeast Ridge II 5.7 Layton Kor, 1959.

ᔕ✓ **44 First Flatiron Baker's Way II 5.2** poor pro.

✓ **45 First Flatiron North Arete II 5.4** poor pro. A beautiful and exciting ridge. Can be started from behind or by climbing Baker's Way (or climb anywhere up East Face 5.2-5.7 poor pro).

Wide Country

The Dome

√**46 Gorilla's Delight I 5.9** Pat Ament and George Hurley, 1965.

47 Supersqueeze I 5.10+ Dave Rearick and Lee Herrell, 1963. FFA: Pat Ament, 1969.

48 The Umph Slot I 5.10 (5.9-5.11 depending on body size) Pat Ament and Wayne Goss, 1964. FFA: Chuck Pratt, 1965.

√**49 Cozyhang II 5.7** Mike O'Brien and Jim Crandle, 1953.

√**50 East Slab I 5.5** The best route on the Dome.

Castle Rock

51 Cussin' Crack II 5.7 Harold Walton and partners, 1950.

52 Jackson's Wall II 5.5 Dallas Jackson and Chuck Merley, 1953.

53 Jackson's Wall Direct II 5.9 George Hurley and Charles Roskosz, 1961. FFA: Layton Kor mid 1960's.

54 Athlete's Feat III 5.10+ Stan Shepard and partners, 1960. FFA complete route: Royal Robbins and Pat Ament, 1964.

55 Country Club Crack II 5.11 Cleve McCarty and Ted Rouillard, 1956. FFA complete route: Pat Ament.

The East Face of Long's Peak photo: Richard DuMais

Lumpy Ridge and Estes Park

ROCKY MOUNTAIN NATIONAL PARK

HIGHLIGHTS

Rocky Mountain National Park holds the most accessible rugged mountains in Colorado and possibly in the United States. Snowfields and, in some cases, alpine tundra are within an arm's length of the parked car, and the climbing has a mountainous flavor that sets it well apart from the standard rock climber's fare. The climbing is principally on excellent granitic rock (though not classic "alpine" granite) and is very diverse in terms of commitment, difficulty and styles demanded. Approach hikes are quite reasonable, allowing most climbs to be done in a one day round trip from the town of Estes Park. Even more popular with rock climbers is Lumpy Ridge, a set of lower altitude crags. The one to six pitch routes are on sun-drenched granite that remains cool even in mid-summer, because of its 8,000 to 10,000 foot elevation.

CLIMBING

Climbing in Rocky Mountain National Park (RMNP) can be split into two completely different realms: the mountains, and Lumpy Ridge.

Though summer climbing in the mountains is almost exclusively on rock, within this genre there is incredible diversity. One can find routes that are almost pure high angle face climbing (especially on Hallet's and in the Cathedral Spires), others that follow crack systems for up to 1,000 feet (notably on the Diamond of Long's Peak), while still others are mostly friction and rounded low-angle face climbing (on the Northwest Face of the Chiefshead).

To climbers worldwide, perhaps the most famous feature of the Park is the Diamond's 1,000 foot, plumb vertical face. It holds numerous difficult free climbs and mixed free and aid routes that are made especially challenging because they begin at an altitude of 13,000 feet; acclimatization is a major consideration in climbing this face.

In addition to the physical effects of altitude, rock climbing in these mountains requires a special respect for the weather. At any time, but especially in early afternoon, thunderstorms with attendant lightning, hail, snow and/or rain can strike. Parties that have over-extended themselves on a route or that are not prepared for the cold and wet will be rudely reminded that mountains are different from crags.

Approaches to climbs range from three to six miles and gain 1,000 to 3,000 feet of elevation. Depending on one's personal taste, approach hikes are done near dawn on the day of the climb, or are done the day before to a bivouac near the base of the route. Only rarely is a rappel descent required; easy backsides are found on each mountain, down which one can walk without trouble.

Because it is less serious and less time consuming, many rock climbers prefer Lumpy Ridge to the mountains. Lumpy's routes are up to seven pitches in length, with some face climbing and some thin slab climbing on the crystals of this rough granite. Most of the routes, however, involve cracks—typically flared and possibly shallow. Climbs are usually less than vertical, though some walls are indeed steep and a few overhangs exist. Since Lumpy Ridge is growing in popularity as a good escape from the mid-summer heat of the Boulder area, crowding is becoming more of a problem. Nevertheless, only the most popular of routes might require waiting for other parties. Few summits at Lumpy require rappel descents, most being walked off from the uphill side of the rock.

Entering RMNP (except for Long's Peak and Lumpy Ridge) costs $2 per car during the summer season, or use a Golden Eagle pass. Climbers driving in for early morning starts will usually find the entrance booths vacant.

ENVIRONMENT

The tasteless tourist town of Estes Park lies in one of Colorado's most

beautiful valleys, with a row of mountains rising to the west, and the crags of Lumpy Ridge protruding from a lightly forested hillside to the north. After passing through Estes Park, the road continues into the Park where one branch becomes Trail Ridge Road—at 12,000 feet, the highest continuous road in the United States—and the other branch leads to the trailheads for several peaks. While treeline lies at roughly 11,000 feet, the coniferous forests are open enough and the mountain walls precipitous enough that beautiful views of glacially carved cirques can be had from many points.

The mountains, including the Continental Divide, are clearly seen from the south facing rocks at Lumpy Ridge. Indeed, the grand views are one of the alluring points of climbing at Lumpy. Additionally, approaching the crags takes one along an exquisite meadowed valley (followed by a short but steep uphill slog), making this a scenic delight among rock climbing areas.

CLIMBING HISTORY

During the early years of exploration, climbing in the Estes Park region focused almost exclusively on Long's Peak—at 14,255 feet, the only summit over 14,000 feet in RMNP. Though likely ascended by Indians to trap eagles for their feathers, the first recorded ascent was in 1868 by a party of surveyors led by Major John Wesley Powell (also the first person to float the Grand Canyon of the Colorado River). Within a few years, a 3rd class route (the Keyhole Route) became extremely popular with tourists and native Coloradans alike. The first exploration of the East Face, considered technical by all routes, was during an epic descent, during which the Reverand Lamb slid down the 1,000 foot snow gully now bearing his name: "Lamb's Slide." As early as 1889 a guidebook was written: *Mountaineering in Colorado: The Peaks about Estes Park*.

But technical climbing did not come to the area (declared a National Park in 1915) until the 1920's. During the 1930's the first professional mountain guide service in Colorado was established to shuffle people up and down the North Face of Long's. To facilitate this, a cable was stretched over the 130 feet of 5.3 climbing that constitutes the only technical section of the route.

During the late 1940's technical climbing was gaining in popularity near the town of Boulder, and people were eager to apply their skills in the mountains. A few climbers explored the crags of Lumpy Ridge and eyed the intimidating Diamond face of Long's. But when two climbers notified the Park Service in 1954 that they planned to climb the Diamond (certainly the most coveted cliff in Colorado) the Park Service forbade the ascent and declared the cliff closed to climbing.

By then interest was starting to spread to the other peaks in the Park, and in 1956 the 1,000 foot North Face of Hallett Peak was climbed. Though its 5.7 climbing was not advanced compared to contemporary climbs in California and the Tetons, it represented a major breakthrough in Colorado.

In 1960, the Park Service re-opened the Diamond, and two Californians were quick to steal the prize (D-1, V 5.7 A4). Incidentally, D-1 takes the most prominent vertical crack line up the center of the Diamond. Because of its historical significance and its compelling line, it was included in the book *Fifty Classic Climbs of North America*. However, reports from climbers generally emphasize the loose rock and unaesthetic climbing; therefore it is not included in this book.

During the 1960's climbing throughout both the mountains and crags

of RMNP skyrocketed in popularity, while the 1970's brought the free climbing revolution into the mountains. Numerous free climbing attempts were made on the Diamond, but it was not until 1975 that success arrived, soon followed by many other freed aid routes.

A special feature of RMNP emerged during the late 1960's and continues to this day: Komito Boots. Few climbing areas have so firmly entrenched a store as a virtual institution. Komito's became an island of sanity for climbers in the otherwise mind-jarring tourist town of Estes Park. Before the re-emergence of guidebooks to the Park in the early 1980s, Komito's was THE place to learn about the routes, and it continues to be the place to buy and resole boots, meet climbers, and stock up on lost equipment.

CAMPING

RMNP is a difficult place to stay for climbers on a tight budget. The major National Park campgrounds, Moraine Park and Glacier Basin, usually require reservations during the prime season. Reservations can be made only between June 30 and August 18; outside of these dates, the campgrounds are first come, first served. They charge $6 per night, have a seven day limit and no showers. For more information, contact RMNP, Estes Park 80517-8397, telephone: 303-586-2371; or the regional office in Denver at 303-236-4648. Reservations can be made from any Ticketron outlet nationwide or from Ticketron Reservations Office, P.O. Box 2715, San Francisco, CA 94126. (There are no phone reservations.)

Other campgrounds in the Park or on National Forest land are always on a first come, first served basis. Olive Ridge, near Allenspark, is about fifteen miles south of Estes Park, but is a good base for Long's Peak climbs. The Long's Peak Campground is at the trailhead and is an even better base. Aspenglen, near Estes Park, is the only National Park campground open all year. They charge $6, have seven day limits, but have no showers.

Several private campgrounds are available, the nicest being the Estes Park Campground, five miles southwest of Estes Park. Showers are available. Telephone: 303-586-4188.

The American Youth Hostel is another convenient option. About ten miles out of town, it provides a shuttle service that passes Lumpy Ridge on its way to Estes. Members $3.75, non-members $5.50. It is only open in summer.

The following places will allow people not staying on their grounds to take showers for a fee: KOA east of town on Highway 34; National Park Resort on Highway 34, four miles west of town.

Grocery stores and all other conveniences can be found in Estes Park. One of several laundromats is found next to the Post Office, downtown on Riverside Drive.

For bivouac information, see *RESTRICTIONS AND WARNINGS*.

SEASONS AND WEATHER
MOUNTAINS

Approximate Months	Typical Temperatures High	Low	Rock Climbing: Likelihood of Precipitation	Frequency of Climbable Days
Nov-Apr	20's	0's	medium	very low
May-Jun	40's+	20's	medium	medium
Jul-Aug	60's	40's−	medium	high-med
Sep-Oct	40's+	20's	med-low	medium

Comments: Afternoon thunderstorms are common in the summer, especially on the Diamond. In the spring and fall, south facing cliffs are generally prefered.

LUMPY RIDGE

Approximate Months	Typical Temperatures High	Low	Likelihood of Precipitation	Frequency of Climbable Days
Nov-Apr	40's−	20's	med-low	low-med
May-Jun	50's+	30's	medium	med-high
Jul-Aug	70's+	50's−	medium	high
Sep-Oct	50's+	30's	med-low	high-med

Comments: Afternoon thunderstorms are common in the summer. Because the rocks face south, snow melts off quickly.

RESTRICTIONS AND WARNINGS

Regulations for climbing in the Park change periodically. It used to be required to sign out for all technical climbs, but at this point that is not necessary. Be aware, however, that this could change, and a fine is imposed for those in violation.

Bivouacing in the Park requires a permit, available free through the Backcountry Office. During the non-summer months, permits can be arranged by telephoning 303-586-2371. During the summer (June 1 to September 30), bivouac permits must be picked up in person at the Backcountry Office (from the parking area for Park Headquarters, follow a path left to a small building in the trees), or by mail (Backcountry Office, Rocky Mountain National Park, Estes Park, CO 80517). They will ask for your climbing plans and the license plate number of the car being left at the trailhead. Since permits to popular areas are in demand, attempt to get yours several days early and be prepared with options in case your prefered dates and places do not work out. Be sure to pick up your permit the day you are scheduled to go out, otherwise any successive nights will be canceled.

In 1985, the following information is applicable for bivouacs.

Criteria: a permit will be issued only if:

1. The site is 3½ miles or more from the trailhead (Hallett Peak and Lumpy Ridge do not qualify).
2. The climb is four or more pitches.

Constraints: These constraints are set up to reduce the sometimes high impact that climbers create through the years. Please heed them.

1. The site must be off of vegetation; you must sleep on rock or snow. Stay off of vegetation around the bivy site if possible.
2. Sites must be 100 feet from water.
3. No tents are allowed. If you use an improvised shelter, do not put it up until dusk, and take it down at dawn. Since only climbers are allowed to bivouac, this regulation reduces their visual impact on non-climbers.
4. The climbing party is limited to four climbers.
5. No fires are allowed; stoves are acceptable.

Restricted sites: In several sites the number of bivouackers is restricted; these sites may be reserved.

Long's Peak: Broadway – 10 people; Chasm View – 6 people

Petit Grepon: Sky Pond – 10 people

GUIDEBOOKS

Lumpy Ridge and other Estes Park Rock Climbs (1985) by Scott Kimball. Available locally from Komito's, or from Chockstone Press, 526 Franklin, Denver, CO 80218.

The High Peaks (1981) by Richard DuMais. The mountainous areas of RMNP. Available locally from Komito's or from Richard DuMais, Box 4804, Boulder, CO 80306.

Fifty Classic Climbs of North America (1979) by Steve Roper and Allen Steck. This covers one route from each of three cliffs. Available locally from Komito's or from Sierra Club Books, 530 Bush Street, San Francisco, CA 94108.

GUIDE SERVICES AND EQUIPMENT STORES

Komito Boots, at 351 Moraine Avenue (on the hill above the Donut Shop, exiting Estes Park towards the main entrance to the Park), sells mountain related footware and guidebooks (open 364 days per year, 9am - 6pm). Upstairs from Komito's is Buzzard Mountainware, selling their own clothing and packs, as well as an adequate line of climbing equipment. The concessionaire for guiding and instruction within Park boundaries is the Colorado Mountain School, PO Box 2106, Estes Park, CO 80517, telephone: 303-586-5758.

EMERGENCY SERVICES

For emergencies in RMNP (including rescues) contact a ranger or call the National Park Service at 911 in an emergency or 586-2371 non-emergency. The Sheriff can be reached at 205 Park Lane, telephone: 586-9511. The only hospital is the Elizabeth Knutsson Memorial Hospital, 555 Prospect Ave, Estes Park, telephone: 586-2317.

GETTING THERE

From Boulder, regular but infrequent bus service is available from the downtown bus station through Gray Line of Estes Park, 231 Moraine Avenue, Estes Park, telephone: 303-586-3301 (Denver phone: 303-289-2841). Hitch-hiking often works well to get to Estes. From Estes Park to the mountains, the Estes Park Bus Company serves the Bear Lake Shuttle parking area. The Bear Lake Shuttle is a free bus available from the Park Service to lessen conjestion at the Bear Lake and Glacier Gorge parking areas—they are usually full during the day. These buses only operate during the day and are useless to climbers starting early and returning late.

John Harlin in RMNP photo: Reinhard Karl

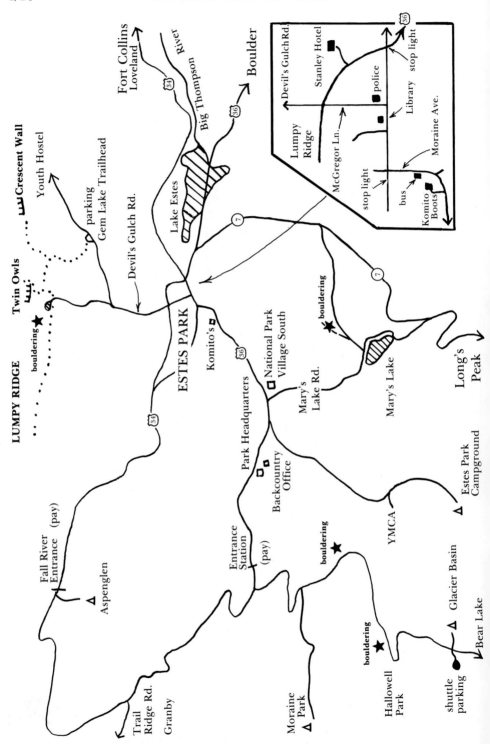

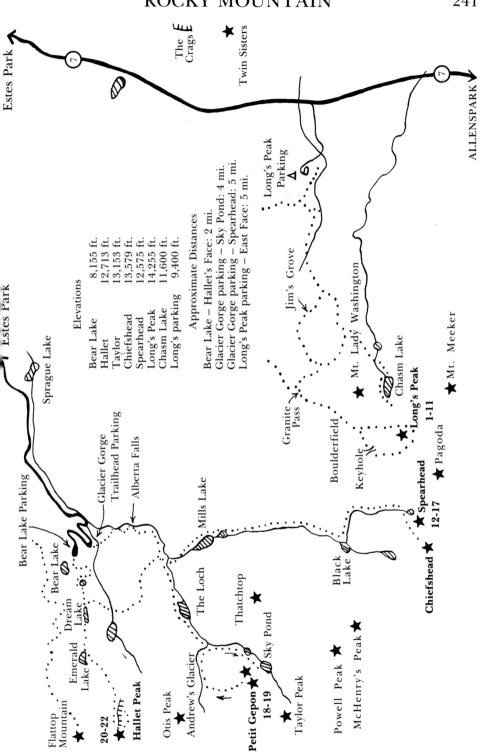

Estes Park

The Crags

Twin Sisters

Estes Park

Allenspark

Long's Peak Parking

Jim's Grove

Elevations

Bear Lake	8,155 ft.
Hallet	12,713 ft.
Taylor	13,153 ft.
Chiefshead	13,579 ft.
Spearhead	12,575 ft.
Long's Peak	14,255 ft.
Chasm Lake	11,600 ft.
Long's parking	9,400 ft.

Approximate Distances

Bear Lake – Hallet's Face: 2 mi.
Glacier Gorge parking – Sky Pond: 4 mi.
Glacier Gorge parking – Spearhead: 5 mi.
Long's Peak parking – East Face: 5 mi.

Sprague Lake

Glacier Gorge Trailhead Parking

Alberta Falls

Mills Lake

Bear Lake Parking

Bear Lake

Granite Pass

Boulderfield

Mt. Lady Washington

Chasm Lake

Long's Peak 1-11

Keyhole

Pagoda

Mt. Meeker

Spearhead 12-17

Chiefshead

Black Lake

The Loch

Thatchtop

Sky Pond

Powell Peak

McHenry's Peak

Flattop Mountain

Dream Lake

Emerald Lake

20-22

Hallet Peak

Otis Peak

Andrew's Glacier

Petit Gepon 18-19

Taylor Peak

Lumpy Ridge

Crescent Wall

1 **Pressure Drop 5.10+ or 5.11−** Dan Hare and Pete Steres. Most parties rappel after 1st pitch. One can continue past bolts (5.11) to overhang and climb to top of wall (Strategic Arms). Last pitch is extremely runout between first and second bolts (placed on rappel).

2 **Finger-Licking Good 5.11−** Scott Woodruff, Brad Gilbert and Dan Hare, 1974.

3 **Crescent Arch 5.11** Ken Duncan, 1977. Wired nuts and 6 in. camming nut helpful.

Twin Owls

Descent: Scramble down notch on north side to chimney (Bowels of the Owls).

✓ **4 Conan's Gonad I 5.9** Larry Bruce and Mark Hesse. Bring 4 in. nut. The striking hand crack in a vertical face. Begins in a stemming chimney.

✓ **5 Organ Pipes II 5.6-5.7** optional 5.9 finish John Chapman and Steve Hickman, 1963. Easiest route stays in corner. Cracks near left side of face are 5.7 and nicer climbing.

6 Wolf's Tooth II 5.8 Tink Wilson and George Lamb, 1958. The chimney on west side of pillar. Nuts to 4 in.

7 Tiger's Tooth II 5.9+ Layton Kor, mid 1960's. The chimney on east side of pillar. Small wires to 4 in. nut.

8 Silly Putty 5.11+(or West Owl Direct A3) Bill Eubank and Brad Van Diver, 1956. FFA: John Bachar and Doug Snively, 1978. Free route has serious runout.

9 Crack of Fear III 5.10+ Layton Kor and Paul Mayrose, 1963 (mostly free). FFA: Chris Fredericks. One of the most notorious routes on Lumpy Ridge—offwidth Ad Nauseum Nuts to 6 in.

10 Peaches and Cream I 5.11 Jim Dunn. Offwidth and lieback. Nuts to 4 inches.

The Book

Descent: 2nd and 3rd class gullys to east.

11 Osiris III 5.7 Dave Johnson and Pete Robinson, 1964.

12 George's Tree I 5.9 (1st pitch) George Hurley and Steve Pomerance, 1967.

13 Fat City to The 44 III 5.10c The 44: Paul Mayrose and Hans Leitinger, 1965, FFA: Billy Westbay, Mark Hesse and Larry Bruce, 1974. Fat City: Bill Forrest and Ray Jardine, 1970. Bring extra tiny stoppers. The classic 5.10 on Lumpy Ridge.

14 Pear Buttress III 5.8+ Layton Kor and partner, 1963. The most popular 5.8 on Lumpy Ridge.

15 J Crack III 5.9+ or 5.11 with headwall Steve Hickman and John Bryant, 1964. FFA headwall: Dan McClure and Billy Westbay, 1974. The classic 5.9 on Lumpy Ridge. Bring extra medium stoppers. The 5.9 version of 3rd pitch has no pro after leaving crack. Middle variation is 5.11.

16 Femp III 5.9 Ren Fenton and Charlie Kemp, 1962.

The Bookmark

Descent: From summit, rappel north to notch, then rappel west.

17 Melvin's Wheel III 5.8+ Bob Bradley and Paul Maryrose, 1965.

18 Romulan Territory III 5.10− Scott Kimball and Bill Wylie.

19 Backflip III 5.9 Steve Shea and Dick Jimmerson, 1969.

The Pear

20 Magical Chrome-Plated Semi-Automatic Enema Syringe III 5.6 Bob Bradley and Paul Mayrose, 1969. Probably the best easy climb on Lumpy Ridge.

21 The Whole Thing II 5.10− Bob Bradley and Paul Mayrose. FFA: Mark Hesse and Larry Bruce, 1974.

22 Right Dihedral II 5.9 Filip Sokol and Jim Sharp, 1968.

Sundance

Approach: Follow trail in valley past fence to dirt road. Walk past dam and buildings in woods about 100 yards, then angle uphill. Avoid open downed aspen groves.

Descent: From Saddle, downclimb and rappel from trees to gully.

Bring plenty of small wired nuts for all routes.

Sundance

23 Mainliner III 5.9 Michael Covington and Wayne Goss, 1972. One of the finest climbs on Lumpy Ridge.

24 Kor's Flake III 5.8 Layton Kor and partner, late 1950's. 4 in. nut, long slings.

25 Mr. President III 5.11 Layton Kor and Steve Komito, late 1950's. FFA: Jeff Lowe and Ron Matous. Named for the devious nature of the route finding.

26 Turnkorner III 5.10 Layton Kor and Jack Turner, early 1960's. FFA: Royal Robbins and Bob Boucher, 1964. Some difficult offwidth.

27 The Nose III 5.10− Filip Sokol, Dick Erb and Jack Jacoba, 1970. FFA: Duncan Ferguson and Chris Reveley.

East Face Long's Peak photo: Richard DuMais

Lower East Face

Long's Peak

Descent: From the summit ridge, descend the North Face. The final low-angle cliff band is usually rappelled from large eye bolts (two 75 ft rappels). To return to the base of the East Face, descend 2nd class talus to the right of the Chasm View Wall (the Camel descent). One can also downclimb **Kiener's**(rt 1) and cross Broadway to pickup bivy gear. To avoid North Chimney in approaching the Diamond, hike to Chasm View and make 3 rappels.

1 Kiener's (Mountaineer's) Route III 5.4 Walter Kiener, Agnes Vaille and Carl Blaurock, 1921. Approximately the line first *descended by Rev. Elkanah Lamb in 1871. Late in the season, crampons help on Lamb's Slide.*

2 Alexander's Chimney III 5.7 W. Zimmerman, 1919.

3 Stettner's Ledges III 5.7 or 5.8 finish Joe and Paul Stettner, 1927.

4 Diagonal V 5.9 A3 Ray Northcutt and Layton Kor, 1959. The pendulum has not been climbed free.

5 Directagonal IV 5.11 Roger and Bill Briggs, 1976.

6 North Chimney II 5.6 E. H. Bruns and W. F. Ervin, 1925. Normal access route to the Diamond. Can be dangerous from rock fall.

The Diamond

7 D-7 V 5.7 C2 or 5.11+ George Hurley, Wayne Goss and Roger Dalke, 1966. FFA: John Bachar and Richard Harrison, 1977. By far the easiest and most popular aid route up the Diamond, but also one of the best and most difficult free routes. Small to medium nuts.

8 Yellow Wall V 5.10+ or 5.8 A3 Layton Kor and Charles Roskosz, 1962. FFA original route: Charlie Fowler and Dan Stone, 1978. Several variations possible for 6th pitch, some are runout and possibly harder than 5.10.

√**9 Casual Route IV 5.10−** Duncan Ferguson and Chris Reveley, 1975. The easiest and most popular free route on the Diamond.

10 Enos Mills 5.8 A3 Layton Kor and Wayne Goss, 1967. Equipment: KB to 4 in., many 1-2 in.

11 Diretissima III 5.10− Layton Kor and Bob Lagrange, 1960. FFA: Roger Briggs. Extra large nuts to 4 inches. The very prominent vertical dihedral/crack system.

Casual Route photo: Phil Mohundro

The Diamond photo: Richard DuMais

Spearhead with McHenry's in background

Steve Komito on Sykes Sickle

The Spearhead

12 Sykes Sickle III 5.7 C1 or 5.10−   Richard Sykes, David Rearick, John Wharton and Dave Işles, 1958. FFA: Royal Robbins, 1964.

13 Barb III 5.10 Walter Fricke and Charlie Logan, 1970. FFA: Dan McClure and Robert Gulley, about 1975. Bring tiny stoppers.

14 North Ridge III 5.6 Peter Roberg and Charles Schobinger, 1958.

Northwest Face of Chiefshead

15 Papoose II 5.8 (5.9 var.) John Harlin and Kent Wheeler, 1980. Usually shaded and cold.

16 Seven Arrows IV 5.10 John Harlin and Charlie Fowler, 1980. Bring many tiny stoppers (nothing larger than 1 in.) and a double sling. Runout, often wet. Start up right edge of large flake leaning against wall.

17 Path of Elders IV 5.10− Layton Kor and Bob Culp, 1961. FFA: Billy Westbay and Dan McClure, 1975. Bring tiny stoppers. Runnout. Many variations possible on upper pitches.

Northwest Face of Chiefshead

The Cathedral Spires

The Petit Grepon

Descents: From Petit Grepon summit, make one long or two short rappels off north edge to saddle, then one more to gully. If bivouac gear has been left near Sky Pond, it may be best to make epic rappels down the gully between the Petit Grepon and the Saber. Better is to climb to notch between Saber and Sharkstooth, then descend by scrambling north to Andrew's Glacier trail.

18 **South Face III 5.8** William Buckingham and Art Davidson, 1961. One of the most popular routes in RMNP (often crowded).

The Saber

19 **Snively-Harlin III 5.10−** Doug Snively and John Harlin, 1980.

The Petit Grepon and the Saber

The Petit Grepon from the North

Hallett Peak

Descent: Hike uphill to the prominent gully, descend gully to fork, scramble up and through gap to left fork, follow this down. Easy 3rd class.

20 Culp-Bossier III 5.8 Bob Culp and Tex Bossier, 1961. Route finding can be tricky.

21 Jackson-Johnson III 5.9 or 5.7 A1 Dallas Jackson and Dale Johnson, 1957.

22 Northcutt-Carter III 5.7 Ray Northcutt and Harvey T. Carter, 1956. The first major technical route in RMNP and still one of the most popular.

Hallett Peak Second Buttress

Hallett Peak Third Buttress

Reynold's Hill

VEDAUWOO

HIGHLIGHTS

Vedauwoo ("vee-da-voo") could be a lost and unheralded twin of the super famous rock climber's winter haven: Joshua Tree. It has one-pitch routes on coarse, crystalline granite domes sprawled over relatively flat and open country. This, combined with the prominence of crack climbs—with a smattering of excellent face routes as well—could be lifted out of Southern California. But when Joshua Tree is basking in mid-winter sunshine, Vedauwoo is smothered by ground blizzards. It is also a diminutive version of the immense Joshua Tree. Still, connoisseurs of crack climbing and expansive views will find a stop at Vedauwoo much to their liking.

CLIMBING

Vedauwoo rocks protrude from their surroundings in individual formations of many sizes and in various shapes, from dome-like to shoe-box-like. The climbing is dominated by a single motif: cracks. Often very steep, and frequently intersected by overhangs, Vedauwoo cracks can exert tremendous resistence to a struggling climber. Couple this with the lacerating crystalline granite, and one can understand the stiff reputation that Vedauwoo often holds with visiting climbers. Still, the routes are short (usually one, occasionally two pitches) and, for lovers of jamming, intensely challenging.

In addition to the cracks, a few high quality face routes exist that climb very thin edges and crystals; these are usually bolt protected. Face climbing is also occasionally encountered while connecting cracks. Approaches are often less than ten minutes from the car, and descents are frequently made by walking off the back-side, though rappelling the route is common.

ENVIRONMENT

Vedauwoo is at the southern end of the Medicine Bow National Forest. As one approaches Vedauwoo from the treeless plains to the south and east, it is difficult to imagine a National Forest here, but the hills of the Laramie Mountains extend to the north from this point and draw sufficient precipitation to support pine forests. The gently rolling country surrounding Vedauwoo (given an Indian name which means "earthborn spirit") supports trees, but from the top of the rocks one sees mostly open plains to the south. In the summer, the only climbing season at this 8,000+ foot elevation, one can often watch thunderheads and rainstorms rolling in from the prairie.

The heart of the Vedauwoo complex is a giant picnic ground set in a small forested valley surrounded by cliffs. Since this is a recreation area just a mile from a major interstate highway and within 20 miles of both Laramie and Cheyenne, picnickers are frequently seen scrambling on the rocks. Still, Vedauwoo could rarely be considered crowded.

CLIMBING HISTORY

Vedauwoo lies just eighteen miles from Laramie, home of the University of Wyoming. As a consequence, students have dominated the development of routes in this area. During the 1960's, a group of serious climbers began free climbing a number of aesthetic and difficult lines, including face climbs in the Fall Wall area. These routes occasionally strayed into the 5.10 range, but many of the vertical cracks were aided rather than pushed free.

In the 1970's, Vedauwoo began attracting attention from Colorado climbers (Boulder is just two hours south). Visiting climbers would occasionally drive up to compete with locals for first ascents and first free ascents. But the notoriety of the crystalline granite, along with a reputation for off-width climbs, kept many Coloradans away. The area continued to be dominated by U.W. students who managed a wealth of first ascents, many of them on classic finger and hand-sized cracks that belied the area's nasty off-width reputation.

By the end of the 1970's and during the early 1980's, hard 5.11 and 5.12 routes were commonplace. Vedauwoo had by then attracted enough attention that most serious climbers visiting Colorado for an extended period would make at least one trip north to crack country. If they didn't, they were missing a wonderful experience, especially when the Front Range of Colorado sweltered in mid-summer heat.

CAMPING

A Forest Service pay campground ($5) is located in the heart of Vedauwoo. Free undeveloped camping can also be found on many of the side roads south and east of the main area. The nearest services are found in Laramie, nineteen miles west.

SEASONS AND WEATHER

Approximate Months	Typical Temperatures High	Low	Likelihood of Precipitation	Frequency of Climbable Days
Nov-Apr	30's	−20's	medium	very low
May-June	50's+	30's+	med-high	low-med
Jul-Sep	70's	50's−	med-low	very high
Oct	50's+	30's	low-med	medium

Comments: Summer precipitation is likely to be in the form of thunderstorms that come and pass quickly.

RESTRICTIONS AND WARNINGS

The nearest telephone for emergency help is a long distance away.

GUIDEBOOKS
Crack Country Revisited (1982) by Layne Kopischka. Available from stores, or Layne Kopischka, 1981 North 17th, Laramie, WY 82070. Routes below 5.10 are often graded stiffly.

GUIDE SERVICES AND EQUIPMENT STORES
The nearest equipment store is Rocky Mountaineering in Laramie.

EMERGENCY SERVICES
In case of emergency, call the Albany County Sheriff at: 911. A phone can be found at the Summit Rest Area (Lincoln Memorial) several miles west on I-80. The nearest hospital is nineteen miles away in Laramie: Ivinson Memorial at 255 North 30th, telephone: 742-2141.

GETTING THERE
Greyhound passes Vedauwoo on I-80, but it is up to the bus driver whether a passenger will be dropped off at this unscheduled stop. Though one cannot leave Vedauwoo by public transportation, hitch-hiking or a ride to town with a climber can usually substitute. Airports can be found in both Laramie and Cheyenne.

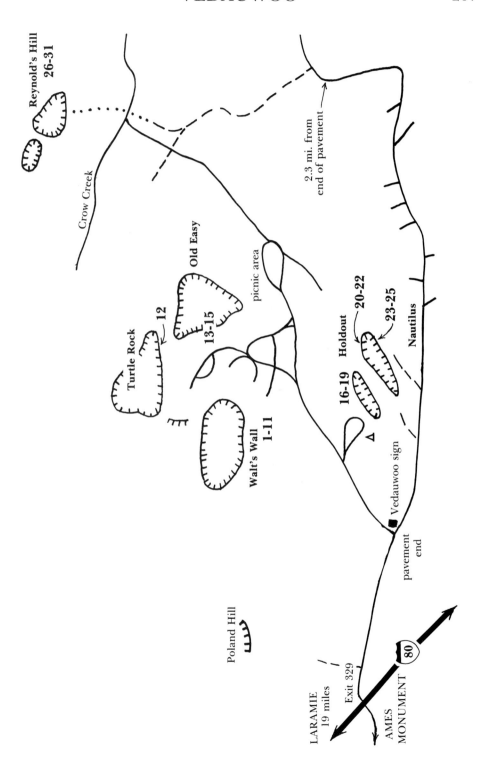

Walt's Wall – Fall Wall Area

1 Edwards Crack 5.6 Jerry Edwards and Ray Jacquot, 1958.

2 Walt's Wall 5.4 First recorded ascent: Walt Stickler, 1954.

3 4th of July Crack 5.12− Mike Covington and partner, 1965. FFA: Todd Skinner and Paul Piana, 1981. The steep dihedral.

4 Horn's Mother 5.11− Rick Horn, 1965. FFA: Dan McClure and Mark Hesse, 1973. The big crack.

5 Board Walk 5.11− Harlan Lahti and John Thomas, 1963. FFA: Tobin Sorenson and partner, 1973.

6 Mainstreet 5.10− Rick Horn and Ned Hallein, 1963. FFA: Mark Hesse and partner, 1972.

7 Spider God 5.11 Paul Piana, 1979.

8 Fall Wall 5.10− Peter Doedt, Keith Becker and Jan Mathiesen, 1965. A large "Friend" is useful to protect before the first bolt.

9 Mickey Mantle 5.10c Doug Cairns, Kim Weaver and Jay Anderson, 1977.

10 5.11 Crack 5.9+ Ken Fisher, 1965. FFA: Mike Parker and Mark Chapman, 1968.

11 Coldfinger 5.7 Peter Koedt and Ken Fisher, 1966.

Hidetaka Suzuki on 4th of July Crack   photo: Michiko Suzuki

Hidetaka Suzuki on Hypertension, Turtle Rock
12 Hypertension 5.12b Mark Wilford and Skip Guerin, 1981.

Old Easy, Mountaineers Rock Climb

13 MRC Direct 5.8+ Original route: Dwight Deal and Peter Sinclair, 1962. Direct: Mike Parker and Roger Howe, 1969.

14 MRC Left 5.7 First recorded ascent: Layne Kopischka and Drew Arnold, 1974. 5.10b variation: Doug Cairns et. al.

15 Right Exit 5.9+ Steve Matous, 1976.

Holdout North Side

Nautilus North End

Nautilus Southeast End

Holdout North Side

16 Reading Raymond Chandler 5.12 − Paul Piana and Mark Rolofson, 1982.

17 Currey's Diagonal 5.10 + /5.11 − Don Currey and partner, early 1960's. FFA: Steve Matous and Doug Cairns, mid 1970's.

18 11 cent Moon 5.11 + Jeb Schenck and Chad Price, 1971. FFA: Paul Piana and Todd Skinner, 1981.

19 Beef Eater 5.10c Ken Fischer and Rodes Moran, 1967. FFA: Larry Bruce and Molly Higgins, 1973.

Nautilus North End

20 Grand Traverse 5.10 + Mark Chapman and Roger Evans, 1968. FFA 1st pitch: Phil Fowler and Dan McClure, 1972. FFA 2nd pitch: Steve Matous and Doug Cairns, mid 1970's.

21 Max Factor 5.11 + Kevin Bein. FFA: Kim Carrigan and Steve Levin, 1980.

22 Bug Squad 5.11c John Sherman and Erik Eriksonn, 1982.

Nautilus Southeast End

23 Friday the 13th 5.11 + FA to first roof: Jan Mathiesen and Jim Halfpenny, 1970. FFA complete route: Todd Skinner and Paul Piana, 1981.

24 Hesitation Blues 5.11 − Nancy Westlund and Bill Hauck, 1970. FFA first pitch (5.11): Doug Cairns, late 1970's. FFA 2nd pitch (5.10): Chick Holtcamp and Bob Yoho, late 1970's.

25 Middle Parallel Space 5.9 Dan McClure and Doug Snively, 1973.

I'd Rather Be in Philadelphia photo: Paul Piana

Reynold's Hill

26 Climb & Punishment 5.9+ Dan McClure and Mark Hesse, 1972.

27 Penis Dimension 5.10c John Garson and Peter Hollis, 1974.

28 Hung Like a Horse 5.11− Gary Pousch and partner, late 1960's. FFA: Ron Matous and Gary Isaacs, 1974.

29 I'd Rather Be in Philadelphia 5.12c Kevin Bein, 1981. FA completed route with loose face traverse left. Lowering off from top of crack (need 165' rope) recommended.

30 Ain't Crack 5.8 Phil Fowler and Keith Goody, 1974.

31 Ain't Crack Headwall 5.9 John Wilke, Steve Gall, et.al., 1979.

Reynold's Hill

The Bridge Area

FREMONT CANYON

HIGHLIGHTS

Isolated in the high plains of central Wyoming lies a granite canyon with climbs that are perhaps unique in Western North America: many are approached by rappelling directly to the route's base, often just above the water's edge. Though the majority of routes here are only one pitch in length, the quality of the climbing makes up for their brevity. There are also longer routes, including 300 feet of vertical climbing on the Power Tower Wall. Rising out of the plains nearby is Dome Rock, with many crack routes and difficult face climbs on its 200 foot exposure. Free undeveloped camping can be found at both areas.

CLIMBING

Most of Fremont Canyon's climbing lies within a half mile of the bridge. Within this short distance, numerous routes of one to three pitches in length lead from the water's edge to the canyon rim. While pure crack climbing dominates many of the routes, Fremont granite is cleaved in clean, perpendicular blocks and is frequently laced with excellent edges and miniature ledges. This gives interesting diversity to the longer routes; crack climbing can be interspersed with sections of face (sometimes runout), and small ledges provide excellent resting spots without compromising the aesthetics of a vertical wall. Because of its steepness, most of the climbing in Fremont Canyon is 5.9 and above in difficulty, though a few good easier routes do exist.

The climbing described in this book falls into three regions. In the

Bridge Area, all the routes are one medium to long pitch in length. These routes are rappelled to, usually by tying a rope around boulders or around the girders of the bridge itself. This rope is left in place, while a second rope is used for leading. Top-roping is sometimes done here—the Canyon lends itself admirably to this—but leading is the norm.

Further east lie the Narrows. Climbs here are usually accessible by walking, and are two to three pitches in length. If the water is high (in the early summer the water level in the dam is frequently kept high), access is problematic. Sometimes a boat is used, sometimes rappels are done, and sometimes the area is left until later.

Slightly further east lies the biggest wall in the canyon: the Power Tower Wall. Three hundred feet tall, this vertical face provides outstanding climbing. The wall is set within the confines of the canyon, but is several hundred feet above the water itself and thus has less of a "sea-cliff" atmosphere than the other cliffs. It also has the longest approach: about a mile of uphill, followed by a walk down a talus-filled gully.

Just west of the Bridge Area lies the West Canyon. Though several routes exist here, only **Wine and Roses**, one of Fremont's finest cracks, is included in this book.

Dome Rock rises out of the cattle-grazed plains that typify most of Wyoming. The granite here is crystalline, though not especially coarse. Unlike much similar granite in the Rocky Mountain Region, face holds tend to be more edge-like than crystal-pinching. The face routes are excellent, though almost universally difficult. However, the cracks offer entertainment for those climbing at a more moderate grade.

ENVIRONMENT

If the water is flowing through Fremont Canyon, usually early season, the sound of the river and the sunlit walls combine for an extraordinary climbing situation. When the water is not flowing, the echoes and the smell of algae along the rocks of the water's edge is at least as special. Though the canyon is typically as deep as it is wide, few climbers feel the sense of entrapment often associated with deep canyons. One does feel isolated in a world of water and rock. The only hint of being in central Wyoming comes from a typical lack of fellow climbers, especially during the week. Another hint might be the sound of coyotes yapping in the evening twilight.

No confusion exists about Dome Rock, however. The expansive views across the plains—barely a tree to be seen—and the Rattlesnake Range rising meagerly to the west are cowboy country all the way. Indeed, even if cowboys are not frequently glimpsed, the cows probably will be—high stepping it on the trail and careful placement of the tent are usually needed.

CLIMBING HISTORY

One of Fremont Canyon's earliest recorded explorations took place when General Fremont made an ill-fated attempt to float the North Platte River. His rafts capsized in a section of the Canyon now buried under the Pathfinder Reservoir (just upstream from the Bridge). Technical climbing in the Rattlesnake Range (which includes the Dome and the Canyon) began in the 1950's when a professor at nearby Casper College organized a climbing club in order to train potential partners. At that time no road led into the currently popular portion of Fremont Canyon, and on their cursory exploration of this region, they found distastefully loose rock. Instead of climbing here, they concentrated on a few domes and faces in the Rattlesnakes that are much less popular today than Dome Rock and Fremont Canyon.

It was not until the early 1970's that a newly formed climbing club took an interest in the Canyon, and in the mid-1970's a few individuals began developing Dome Rock. Routes in the earlier 1970's often used aid whenever the grade became harder than 5.8, but by the late 1970's locals were climbing 5.10. Not until the early 1980's did a few locals begin a new route explosion; especially in the Canyon, vast quantities of lines remained to be climbed.

The 5.11 standard became firmly established in 1982, and within a year a guidebook and several magazine articles were published. The attention prompted occasional visits from travelling climbers—almost unheard of before. Locals, with occasional help from the visitors, doubled the number of routes in the canyon in two seasons.

CAMPING

Both the Dome and Fremont Canyon are on Bureau of Land Management (BLM) land. Camping is permitted and is free, though completely undeveloped. More developed campsites can be found by the lakeside within a few miles of the climbing. Showers, laundry, and city amenities are found in Casper, forty miles east, though some groceries, gasoline, and camping supplies can be found at Sloane's Store, at the turnoff in Alcova.

SEASONS AND WEATHER

Approximate Months	Typical Temperatures High	Low	Likelihood of Precipitation	Frequency of Climbable Days
Nov-Mar	20's	0's	medium	very low
Apr-Jun	60's	30's	medium	medium
Jul-Aug	70's +	50's	low	very high
Sep-Oct	60's +	30's	medium	medium

RESTRICTIONS AND WARNINGS

While exploring for new rock outside of the mentioned areas, be sure to close local ranchers' gates and ask permission where appropriate. Since climbing accidents are virtually unprecedented in the Casper region, local rescue services are little trained in cliff evacuations. Other than occasional runouts and loose rock, the only hazard to watch out for is the illusive rattlesnake.

GUIDEBOOKS

High Plains Climbs (1983) by Patrick Parmenter, Kelly Moore, and Arno Ilgner. Available from stores or Patrick Parmenter, 137 Harvey Place, Casper, WY 82601. Although the book is generally accurate and useful, the number of routes in the Canyon almost doubled within a year of publication.

GUIDE SERVICES AND EQUIPMENT STORES

Mountain Sports, at 543 South Center Street, in Casper, is the local climbing equipment store. They often have a list of local climbers from which one may make contacts to go climbing.

EMERGENCY SERVICES

The nearest phone is found in Alcova, ten miles from Fremont Canyon. From here one can contact the Natrona County Sheriff at 234-1581, or 911 in case of an emergency. The nearest hospital is Natrona County Memorial at 1233 East 2nd Street, telephone: 577-7201.

GETTING THERE

Public transportation by bus or airplane is available to Casper, where one can rent a car. Hitch-hiking is reasonable as far as Alcova, but traffic is light beyond there. On a weekend morning, displaying a climbing rope may help to snag a climber's car. Better still, consult the list of phone numbers at Mountain Sports.

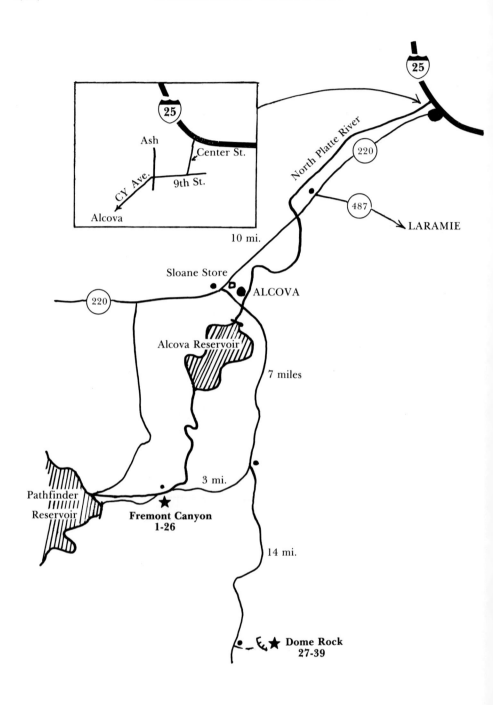

Ash

Center St.

CY Ave.

9th St.

Alcova

10 mi.

North Platte River

220

487

LARAMIE

Sloane Store

ALCOVA

220

Alcova Reservoir

7 miles

3 mi.

Pathfinder
Reservoir

Fremont Canyon
1-26

14 mi.

Dome Rock
27-39

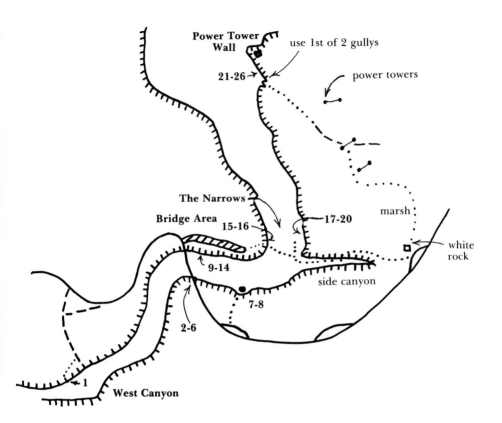

Power Tower Wall

use 1st of 2 gullys

21-26

power towers

The Narrows

Bridge Area

15-16

17-20

marsh

white rock

9-14

side canyon

7-8

2-6

1

West Canyon

Wine and Roses photo: Arno Ilgner

West Canyon
  1 **Wine and Roses 5.11 −**   FFA: Steve Petro and Arno Ilgner, 1984.

South Rim under Bridge
  2 **Bushwacker 5.9**
  3 **Bridge Route 5.8** Dunlap Variation 5.8 Jim Dunlap and Kelly Moore, 1976.
  4 **Escape 5.8**
  5 **Dillingham Blues 5.10b** Arno Ilgner and Steve Petro, 1982.
  6 **All Time Loser 5.11 −** Arno Ilgner and Steve Petro, 1982.

Fremont Pinnacle (South Rim Bridge Area) photo: Arno Ilgner

7 North Face 5.9+ Jim Dunlap and Kelly Moore, about 1978.

8 Silverheels 5.11 Arno Ilgner, 1983.

Easy Day Area (North Rim Bridge Area) photo: Arno Ilgner

9 Imjin Scout 5.10− Arno Ilgner and Kelly Moore, 1984. First ascent was done without bolt. Even with bolt, runout at crux.

10 Easy Day For A Lady 5.8+ FA: unknown.

B-25 Wall photo: Arno Ilgner
11 B-25 Wall 5.9 — Pat Parmenter and Kurt Breuer, 1982.
12 Stone King 5.8 + Arno Ilgner and Steve Petro, 1984.
13 Hemateria Left 5.7 Jim Cunningham and Pat Parmenter, 1983.
14 Greystoke 5.10c Arno Ilgner and Kelly Moore, 1984.

Robert Peterman starting Stone King

Robert Peterman on Stone King

Sun Buttress Area (The Narrows)

15 Welcome Back/Ranger One 5.10— Ron Radzietta and Dave Holsworth, 1979. FFA: Steve Petro and Arno Ilgner, 1983.

16 Red Rover 5.10+ Arno Ilgner and Pat Parmenter, 1982. FFA: Arno Ilgner and Steve Petro, 1982.

Slab Buttress Area (The Narrows)

17 **Slab Route 5.10−** Jack Riley and Carl Kreigerscott, about 1975. FFA: Kelly Moore, Jim Dunlap and Dave Holsworth, 1978.

18 **Potentially Kinetic 5.10+** Arno Ilgner and Kelly Moore, 1982.

19 **Bubble Gum 5.11+** Steve Petro and Kelly Moore, 1983. FFA: Mark Wilford, 1983.

20 **Second Dihedral 5.9** Pat Parmenter and Steve Petro, 1979.

Power Tower Wall
21 Fail Safe 5.9− Arno Ilgner and Kelly Moore, 1982.
22 Block Busters 5.8 Arno Ilgner and Kelly Moore, 1982.
23 High Cost of Climbing 5.9 Arno Ilgner and Ted Ware, 1983.

24 **Sword of Damocles 5.11b** Arno Ilgner and Steve Petro, 1984.
25 **Journeyman 5.11−** Arno and Mark Ilgner, 1983.
26 **Power Tower Route 5.10−** Ron Radzietta and Charlie King, about 1980. FFA: Arno Ilgner and Kelly Moore, 1982.

Dome Rock

Dome Rock East Face   photo: Arno Ilgner
36 Colorado Cake Walk 5.9 Dave Holsworth and Debbie Bergland, 1978.
   Meathead Variation 5.10+, Bill Alexander and Kelly Moore, about 1979.
37 Precambrian Squeeze 5.10− Ron Radzeitta and Pat Parmenter, 1979.
38 Thin Tin 5.10+ Arno Ilgner and Steve Petro, 1982.
39 Wind Jammer 5.9 Pat Parmenter, Steve Petro and Kelly Moore, 1981.

Dome Rock South Face

27 The Thumb 5.8 Bob Scarpelli, about 1974. Bring large nuts.

28 Aqua Lung 5.11b Arno Ilgner and Steve Petro, 1983. 5 bolts.

29 Vector Factor 5.8+ Pat Parmenter and Steve Splittgerber, 1979.

30 Durrance Deja Vu 5.6 Pat Parmenter and Shawn Hogan, 1976. Bring large nuts or tube chocks.

31 Wire Brush 5.10c Steve Petro, roped solo 1980. FFA: Arno Ilgner and Steve Petro, 1982.

32 Skaane 5.10c Arno Ilgner and Steve Petro, 1984.

33 St. Olav 5.10− Arno Ilgner, 1983. The first ascent was made without the bolts.

34 Troll's Handshake 5.11− Arno Ilgner and Steve Petro, 1982.

35 Climbing Lessons 5.5 Finger crack. Pat Parmenter solo, 1980.

The Cathedral Spires

NEEDLES

HIGHLIGHTS

Those with a prejudice against the flat monotony of the Midwest will find it ironic that one of North America's most beautiful and unique climbing areas lies in South Dakota. The rolling, forested Black Hills are home to an incredible collection of rock spires that almost require the name "Needles" because of their pointed summits. The granite of these spires is so coarse-grained that sometimes the crystals can actually be tied off for protection. The roughness can be unnerving to anyone considering taking a leader fall, but even more unnerving is the frequent runout nature of the climbing. Though camping is available within walking distance of the routes, climbers must compete for tent space with millions of other tourists who visit this historically rich and aesthetically beautiful area. Fortunately, many of the tourists are diverted from the camping and climbing areas by the small towns scattered through the countryside.

CLIMBING

While the Pinnacles of California offer a few sharply pointed summits, no popular climbing area in North America has anything approaching the quantity of truly needle-like spires as the Black Hills. Though the Needles range up to 400 feet in height, they average closer to one pitch in length (the larger ones also become more blocky and less pointed).

   Climbing at the Needles is unusual, and not everyone enjoys it initially. Despite the fact that the rock is granite, its gigantic crystalline nature makes it very different from the granite most climbers are accustomed to. The climbing is somewhat like that of the better known Pinnacles in California, only the rock is generally sound; even precarious looking projecting crystals are usually solid. Cracks exist, but they are not common. Jamming can be compared to holding open a pirhana's mouth with bare hands (tape is frequently used when climbing cracks). The same type of crystals and sharply cut knobs that can make jam cracks painful supply face holds that cover each needle. The difficulty of climbing is usually a function of the size and spacing of available crystals.

The other difficulty in climbing at the Needles is psychological but based on a very physical premise. Runouts are often long and the consequences of a fall can be painful. The runout nature comes from a long standing tradition at the Needles of doing only free climbs, and only protecting those climbs free and on the lead. Since standing around to drill a bolt hole on the steep blank faces is often difficult, few bolts have been placed. The scarcity of bolts is also partly due to the talented group of climbers responsible for many of the first ascents. New hard routes are often being better protected, though still on the lead. Sometimes protection can be found by tying off projecting crystals. On steep routes, a simple push out from the wall will often keep the falling climber from getting scraped skin.

A reputation for poor protection frightens many climbers into never visiting the Black Hills. However, there is a simple remedy for those who care more about the joy of climbing than the ego of decimals: lower your sights. Instead of attacking 5.10, enjoy a 5.6. One can always work back up the grades according to taste and experience.

Approaches can be as short as stepping out of the car or as long as a mile's walk on gentle terrain.

The summits of the spires are rarely cluttered with rotting rappel slings. Where a natural horn to double the rope around is not present, the traditional descent technique is as follows: the first person down rappels using the person on the summit as an anchor. The first person then holds the end of the rope or ties it off on the ground while the summit person drapes the other end of the rope (or the second rope) down the opposite side of the spire. He then rappels down that side. Naturally, one must be careful to place the rope in a spot from which it is unlikely to roll. Also, it must be noted that this abrasive technique is rough on ropes. Lately, local climbers have been placing permanent rappel anchors on many summits to avoid the unsightly slings frequently left by visiting climbers.

Summit registers are found on top of most of the Needles. Climbers are very strongly urged to not remove these historical markers or anything inside of them; locals maintain them for a record of the area.

The routes described in this book can only cover a fraction of the many excellent areas within the Needles. Besides the roadside climbing on the Needle's Eye and the Ten Pins, the Cathedral Spires were chosen because their wild and beautiful nature seems to exemplify the allure of the Needles. Local climbers, however, spend much of their time at the numerous other areas. To aid the visitor, some locals have provided the following recommended route list (descriptons can be found in the local guidebooks):

FAR DOWNS – MIDDLE EARTH
Gateway to Mordor, 5.10; Shelob, 5.9; Right Wing of Smog, 5.7; Left Wing of Smog, 5.11; Adventures of Bilbolting Baggins, 5.8

OUTLETS
Youbet Jorasses Rock: Inner Course, 5.2 Inner Outlet: Cold Feat, 5.7; Retable Route, 5.6; Kamp's Crack, 5.7; Hardrocker, 5.9 **Outer Outlet:** Conn Diagonal Traverse, 5.6; Jugs, 5.9; Nick of Time, 5.9+/5.10− **Vertigo View:** Ocean Gypsy (variation), 5.7; Sex Never Did This To My Hands, 5.9 **Old People's Dome:** Barber's Dihedral, 5.8 **Young People's Dome:** Michael's Crack, 5.8 **Vertigo:** 5.11+

PHOTOGRAPHER'S ROCK AREA
Aquarian Rock: Regular Route, 5.3; Four Little Fishies, 5.9 **Photographer's Peak:** Impulse, 5.8

NEEDLE'S EYE AREA
Fan: Moonlight Rib, 5.2 **Thimble:** Regular Route, 5.3 **Gnoman:** Doody Direct, 5.7/5.8 **Wendy:** 5.7 **Exclamation Point:** Route Two, 5.7 **Bloody Spire:** Regular Route, 5.6 **Sore Thumb:** 5.9 **John's Jump:** Shredded Wheat, 5.11− **Special K:** 5.11 **Holey Terror:** Julius Seizure, 5.10

TEN PINS AND SWITCHBACKS AREAS
Leaning Tower: 5.2 **Falcon:** Regular Route, 5.7, Prelude to Orgasm, 5.11 **Reunion Rock:** Trojan Determination, 5.8 **Dave's Dinghy:** Regular Route, 5.9−, Head's You Win, 5.9 **Moby Dick:** Nantucket Sleighride, 5.10; Regular Route, 5.3 **Pawn:** Patience, 5.8 **Sandberg Peak:** North Route, 5.8 **November Mine:** Outer Limits, 5.6 **Split Pin:** No Holds Barred, 5.10

ENVIRONMENT

The Black Hills defy any stereotyped image of South Dakota. Though surrounded by flat wheat and corn fields, the Black Hills are rolling, forested and exquisitely beautiful. The pine forests hold small, crystal clear streams and occasional reservoirs (notably Sylvan Lake, near the cliffs). The Needles are in a small extension of Custer State Park; the larger portion is somewhat south and is a game preserve, featuring herds of bison, elk, and pronghorn antelope.

Like at nearby Devil's Tower, the roadside climbing, especially at the Needle's Eye Area, is plagued by tourists. They often can't understand that answering their shouted questions is not more important than negotiating the crux of a climb. The Needle's Eye Area should only be climbed in a good state of humour and very early in the morning or in the evening. Outside of the Custer State Park boundaries, travellers are confronted with the most amazing concentration of tourist traps that anyone can wish to avoid.

While these tourists undoubtedly enjoy the beauty of the Black Hills, the majority have come especially to view the gigantic portraits of four U.S. Presidents carved into the granite mountainside of nearby Mt. Rushmore. Also nearby is another monument, even larger and more interesting because it is still in the early stages of being carved. Crazy Horse Monument is also one of the few tributes to the Indians in this land of General Custer. Another attraction, about fifty miles further east, is the Badlands National Park. A desolate, moon-like land of dry, sedimentary canyon mazes, this country could not be a greater contrast to the lushness of the Black Hills.

CLIMBING HISTORY

The earliest climbing explorations into the Needles began in the 1930's with the establishment of the the Wiessner Route on Inner Outlet. During the late 1940's and 1950's an energetic couple moved into the Black Hills and became the first and foremost serious Needles climbers. Making over 200 first ascents, most of them to virgin summits, they were anxious to share their private climbing area with whomever they could persuade to pass through. By the 1960's, a few Midwesterners, Northeasterners and Californians were making regular month-long visits to the Needles during the prime midsummer climbing season. The few people who climbed regularly in the Needles were at the top of contemporary standards, and because of the bold climbing style required, some of their routes still see very few ascents.

Even though they were climbing at a very high level of difficulty—reason enough for many to relax their ethics—Needles climbers maintained the tradition of placing protection (including the occasional bolt) free and on the lead. It was felt that a spire ascended with aid had not been climbed.

During the 1970's climbing at the Needles was discovered by an increasing number of locals and outsiders. The few remaining virgin summits were reached, and many more hard climbs were established. Most of the early climbers faded away, while an increasingly mobile climbing community moved in—or rather, passed through. By the early 1980's, climbers would travel for great distances to participate in annual Climb-A-Thon celebrations, with top ropes strung from many of the spires and kegs of beer flowing freely. The tradition has not been maintained of late, but might come back.

CAMPING

A number of camping options exist in the Needles area, but the most popular is the Sylvan Lake Campground ($7). Excellent bouldering is available within a half mile. The principal climbing cliffs can also be reached on foot. Nevertheless, most lazy climbers drive. Coin-operated showers are available ($0.25). A small general store and restaurant are located nearby at Sylvan Lake but are open only during the summer months. The nearest laundry is in Custer. Innumerable private camp-grounds are available within a short drive. Also, in the National Forest outside of Custer State Park, one can find free out of the way spots. Locals will often direct visitors to free camping IF THESE SPECIAL PLACES ARE WELL MAINTAINED AND NOT TRASHED OUT. A South Dakota Parks pass is worth its price ($12) if several day visits are planned; otherwise pay the $3 daily entrance fee.

SEASONS AND WEATHER

Approximate Months	Typical Temperatures High	Low	Likelihood of Precipitation	Frequency of Climbable Days
Nov-Mar	30's	20's	medium	med-low
Apr-Jun	50's	30's	high	low-med
Jul-Aug	70's+	50's	low-med	high
Sep-Oct	50's−	30's−	med-low	med-high

Comments: Some summers can stay wet for long periods, while some winters can offer good, albeit cold, climbing weather. 50 degree days are not uncommon in winter.

RESTRICTIONS AND WARNINGS

The State Park imposes no restrictions on climbing, except that if climbers continue being a spectacle (causing traffic jams) in the Needle's Eye Area, it may be closed to climbing. Be prepared to turn back if a runout seems too long.. Some older bolts require thin carabiners.

GUIDEBOOKS

Touch the Sky: The Needles in the Black Hills of South Dakota (1983) By Paul Piana. Good history and verbal descriptions. Available locally from Mountain Goat Sports in Rapid City and (also by mail) Bob Archbold, 602 St. James, Rapid City SD 57701. Also from the American Alpine Club, 113 East 90th St, New York, NY 10028. *A Poorperson's Guidebook: Selected Free Climbs of the Black Hills Needles* (1984) By Dingus McGee and the Last Pioneer Woman. Available locally or from Dennis Horning, Poorperson's Guidebooks, RR1 Box 88-Y, Custer S.D. 57730. Contains no historical information or photos, but is very cheap and adequately functional.

GUIDE SERVICES AND EQUIPMENT STORES
A local guide service is Reach For the Sky Mountaineering, Bob Archbold, 602 St. James, Rapid City, SD 57701, telephone: 605-343-2344. The nearest equipment store is Mountain Goat Sports, 2111 Jackson Blvd, and Sports World, in the Baker Park Shopping Center, Rapid City.

EMERGENCY SERVICES
In case of emergency, contact a Park ranger or call Custer County Sheriff at 643-4467. The nearest hospital is the Custer Community Hospital located next to the Clinic at 1041 Montgomery, Custer; telephone hospital: 673-2229, clinic: 673-2201.

GETTING THERE
Trailways buses leave daily (morning) from Rapid City to Custer. Air and bus transportation can be taken to Rapid City, from which a car can be rented. Hitch hiking, even from Custer, is not likely to be very efficient, but once one is at the Sylvan Lake Campground, a car is not necessary to reach the climbs.

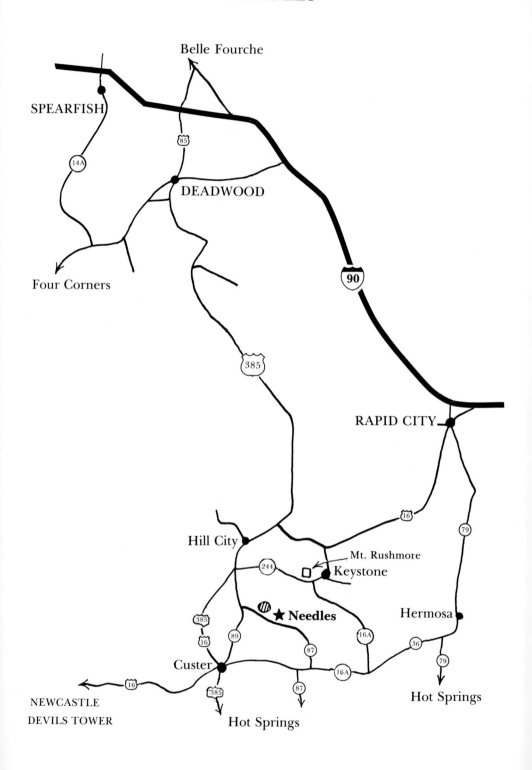

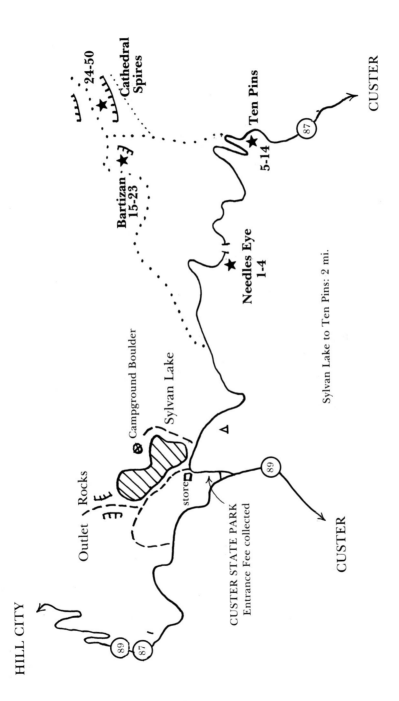

24-50

Cathedral
Spires

Bartizan
15-23

Ten Pins

5-14

87

CUSTER

Needles Eye
1-4

Sylvan Lake to Ten Pins: 2 mi.

Campground Boulder

Sylvan Lake

Outlet Rocks

store

89

CUSTER STATE PARK
Entrance Fee collected

CUSTER

HILL CITY

89 87

Bell Tower and Needle's Eye

The Needle's Eye

Bell Tower and Needle's Eye

Routes 1 and 2 should not be climbed when many tourists are present. Two ropes needed for rappels from all routes.

1 **5.8** Rich Goldstone and Don Storjohann, 1964. Start downhill and climb up as if going into the Eye, then traverse right to edge and gain flake. Serious runout 2nd pitch!

2 **5.9+/5.10** Renn Fenton year unknown. Poor pro; controversial bolt may have been removed.

3 **Every Which Way But Loose 5.10** Pete deLanoy, Paul Muehl, Paul Piana and Mark Smedley, 1979.

4 **Kamp's Crack 5.10** Bob Kamps and Rich Goldstone, 1967.

The Ten Pins, from uphill

5 Energy Crisis 5.11 (Deception Pinnacle) Kevin Bein and Barbara Devine, 1980.

6 End Pin 5.10+ Roger Wiegand and Pete Cleveland, 1970. FFA: Rich Goldstone and Dick Williams, 1975. Climb corner nearest road past 2 bolts.

7 Quartz Jester 5.10 or 5.11+ Henry Barber and Dennis Horning, 1978; direct variation: Kevin Bein, 1981.

8 Kingpin 5.8/5.9 Herb and Jan Conn, 1952. Climb the line of least resistance; originally 5.7 before broken hold.

9 Queenpin 5.9 or 5.10− Royal and Liz Robbins, Dick Laptad and Sue Prince, 1964.

The Ten Pins, from downhill

10 Tricouni Nail (Cerberus) 5.8 Royal and Liz Robbins, Dick Laptad and Sue Prince, 1964. Superb route.

11 Superpin 5.10 Henry Barber, Dennis Horning and Chip Lee, 1977. FA of spire (via no pro 5.11 route): Pete Cleveland, 1967. Runout. Rock may be less good than other Pins (crystals break).

12 Tent Peg 5.7 Royal and Liz Robbins, 1964.

13 Safety Pin 5.6 John Gill and Bob Kamps, 1967.

14 Hairy Pin 5.10+ Pete Cleveland, 1967. Only 1 bolt below shoulder; 15+ feet 5.10 past bolt, then more hard climbing. Serious runout!

The Tent Peg photo: Dan Hare

Perry Williams descending Queen Pin

Bartizan Wall

15 The Naked Rib 5.10 Paul Muehl and Pete deLanoy, 1982. All bolt pro. 1st
pitch 5.10 runout; 2nd pitch 5.9 with only 1 bolt.

16 Crack of Earthly Delights 5.9 Jim Black, Pete deLanoy and John Matteson,
1980. Descent: 30 ft rappel west, stem north, scramble down.

17 Terror-Cracktyl 5.9 Steve Levin, Jim Black, Bob Archbold and Rich Cordes,
1980.

18 **Angry Morning 5.9** Bob Archbold and Jim Black, 1980.

19 **Thanatos 5.12 −** Kevin Bein, Sam Slater, Jim Waugh and Bruce Thompson, 1980.

20 **Window of the West 5.11 −** Sam Slater and Bruce Thompson, 1980.

21 **Bartizan (Kevizan) 5.10 +** Steve Wunsch and John Bragg, 1977.

22 **Elrod's Epic 5.9** Bob Archbold and Elrod Williams, 1981.

23 **Afternoon Delight 5.7** Bob Archbold, Jay Ellwein and Todd Van Alstyne, 1980.

The Cathedral Spires

The Cathedral Spires

Note: The same route will often appear on several different photos.

24 Friend of the Devil 5.8 Pete deLanoy, Bob Archbold and Brian Sarni, 1980. Climb to and through bombay chimney to small ledge with fixed piton, face climb right to crack to route 25.

25 5.9 John Gill, 1964.

26 5.5 Herb and Jan Conn, 1952. Finger crack right of chimney provides better climbing and pro.

27 God's Own Drunk 5.8+ Howie Richardson, Jim Kanzler and an Englishman, 1971. The large dihedral on Khayyám Spire.

28 Moving Finger 5.3 Herb and Jan Conn, 1953.

29 Tower of Darkness 5.3 Herb and Jan Conn, 1953.

30 5.8 Herb and Jan Conn, 1952.

31 Paradise Enow 5.10+ Paul Muehl, Tom Young and Dave Hashisaki, 1981.

32 Blue-Eyed Siberian Husky 5.9 Bob Archbold and Mark Ebel, 1978. Starts next crack left of route 33.

33 Possibly Not 5.7 by normal start, 5.8 by route 32 crack. Brian Sarni, Bob Archbold and John Driscoll, 1979.

34 Wildman Traverse 5.7 Paul Piana, Ken Jones and Chris Field, 1971.

35 Chip's Shit 5.10 Bob Archbold and Chip Devereaux, 1979.

36 5.6 John Dudra and Fred Beckey, 1952. FFA: Herb and Jan Conn. Runout on easier rock.

37 5.6 Barry Corbet, Jake Breitenbach and Charles Plummer, 1956. Climb crack to top.

38 Spire Two 5.3 Herb and Jan Conn, 1949 (this may be the line taken by Bill House, Fritz Wiessner and Lawrence Coveney in 1937; the first of the Cathedral Spires to be climbed).

39 Cat's Meow 5.9+ Bob Archbold and Todd Van Alystyne, 1980. Line of last pitch approximate: follow seam of crystals past bolt to crack.

40 Aku Aku 5.9 Dick Laptad and Sue Prince, 1965. FFA: Mark Powell, Dave Rearick and Bob Kamps, 1966.

41 Thunder Rock 5.5 Herb and Jan Conn and Chuck Nauman, 1953.

42 Freak's Fright 5.10 Bob Kamps and Rich Goldstone, 1967.

43 Freak's Foot 5.8 Mark and Beverly Powell and Bob Kamps, 1966.

44 Teeter-Totter Tower 5.7 Herb and Jan Conn, 1954.

45 5.7/5.8 Herb and Jan Conn, 1953. Requires thin carabiners for bolts.

46 5.4 Herb and Jan Conn, 1948. Begin at back of wide chimney.

47 East Gruesome 5.8 Herb and Jan Conn, 1959. Guidebooks have traditionally not described the line of this fine and intricate route (put up in tennis shoes and with a 50 foot rope).

48 Laptad Route 5.9 Dick Laptad, Paul Muehl, Dave Emery and Julie McFarland, 1979.

49 Eye Tooth 5.8 Bob Kamps and Mark and Beverly Powell, 1962.

50 5.9 Mark and Beverly Powell and Bob Kamps, 1964.

The Cathedral Spires

esome
)some

East

Spire Five

48

Empire State
Building

5.7

5.9+

Teeter-Totter
Tower

Aku Aku

44

Freak's
Foot

50

Thunder Rock

Freak's
Fright

5.8

Flying
Buttress

40

41

42

43

The Cathedral Spires

The Cathedral Spires

South Tower

Spire Four

Spire Three

45

46

Sputnik

5.8

5.7

5.8

5.7

45

46

45

chim
3rd

48

47

West
Gruesome

East

49

Eye Tooth

39

Teeter-Totter

Aku Aku

44

Freak's Foot

5.8

Flying Buttress

40

43

The Cathedral Spires

Freak's Fright

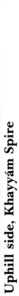

Uphill side, Khayyám Spire

South Tower

Perry Williams on South Tower

Devils Tower

DEVILS TOWER

HIGHLIGHTS

Rising abruptly out of the surrounding plains and forest, the Devils Tower is so spectacular that it was made America's first National Monument. Its summit is 900 feet higher than the encircling tourist-jammed trail, but it is the last 500 feet that are uniformly shear. The columnar structure of this superb rock (phonolit porphry) provides almost monotonously consistent crack climbing of all sizes and difficulties. Because cliffs are available on every side of the Tower, climbers can seek out or avoid the sun at their pleasure, rendering climbing possible almost year-round with good weather.

CLIMBING

Devils Tower was a molten igneous volcanic neck that formed almost perfect hexagonal columns as it cooled. Granite-like, but even harder, the rock is split by hundreds of vertical cracks that run the entire height of the face. On the South Face, routes climb less than 300 feet before reaching the Meadows, a large grass and bush covered ledge, from which one can third class to the summit. Other faces rise nearly vertically for 500 feet to the summit plateau.

As the surrounding landscape eroded from around the Tower, it hesitated for a few millennia about one-third of the way from the summit. This section, which was exposed to the elements much longer than the lower two-thirds of the crag, is somewhat more decomposed than the perfect rock below. For this reason, many climbers prefer to rappel after the best climbing instead of continuing to the summit.

Face climbing is rare on the Tower, but cracks of all sizes abound. The perfection and length of the cracks can make them tedious to some climbers who become bored with the repetitious moves; others find delight in the very same qualities. Stemming between columns adds the diversity of burning calves to the pain of toe jams.

Because the easiest way up the rock is 5.7, all descents are by rappel. The Park Service has established superb bolt anchors for the Meadows Rappel, and it is used as the standard rappel route for all descents from the summit. It requires two 150 foot ropes. Many routes at the Tower (but not the **Durrance**) require 165 foot ropes to reach established belay stations.

ENVIRONMENT

The plains of north-eastern Wyoming were home to the Sioux Indians until the arrival of the U.S. Army and cattle ranchers in the mid 1800's. This country has the broad, unforested valleys and wooded hills that attracted homesteaders. Then the dramatic Devils Tower was used as a landmark for homesteader get-togethers. Today, it teams with the Black Hills of South Dakota, like twin stars, to pull vast numbers of vacationers out of the open space of the Midwest.

The impact of all these tourists on climbers is significant. Nowhere in America—Yosemite included—is one so inundated with questions and comments. The rangers even hold frequent climbing equipment demonstrations and have a booklet for sale entitled *How Do They Get Their Ropes Up There?* Rather than experience the frustration and eventual rudeness brought on by a barrage of questions from well-intentioned onlookers, many climbers soon learn to hide their gear in packs.

CLIMBING HISTORY

According to Indian myth, the first ascent of the Devils Tower occured when seven Indian maidens jumped onto a low rock to escape a pursuing grizzly bear. They prayed to the rock to save them, prompting it to grow to its present height. The visible cracks are said to be claw marks left by the bear, while the seven maidens have now taken their heavenly place as the star formation known as the Pleiades.

Once so many adventurous frontiersmen started gathering at the base of the Tower, it is not surprising that they eventually devised a way to climb it. Two ranchers drove wooden stakes into one of the cracks, forming a crude, yet ingenious ladder upon which they could ascend the sheer wall. They saved their final summit bid until a huge Fourth of July celebration in 1893 when they planted the American flag on the summit to the cheers of the throng below. Several dozen people climbed the Tower via this ladder until in 1928 the lower 100 feet was removed because it had deteriorated so badly. The upper section was left for its historical significance.

The first free ascent was made in 1937 by what has become known as the **Wiessner Crack**. This 5.7 route was then one of the hardest technical climbs in the country. The **Durrance Route**, climbed the next year, is technically somewhat easier and has since become the most popular way up the Tower. During this early climbing history, permission had to be granted from Park Service Headquarters in Washington D.C. This bureaucratic hassle, combined with the Tower's remote location, limited ascents until the late 1950's. The most celebrated climb came in 1941 when a parachutist landed on the summit—and was rescued by climbers five days later. In 1983 an unknown individual climbed the Tower and dived off with a parachute, thus completing the jump forty-two years later.

The **Durrance** and the **Wiessner Routes** were the only ones on the Tower until 1951. In 1956, climbers were invited to participate in the 50th anniversary of the National Monument. Most of the new routes established during this period were "nail-ups" by army teams. Many of these climbs have long been forgotten; occasional "new routes" still run across rusting army ring-angle pitons.

The majority of the routes that were gradually added to the Tower were artificial climbs. During the 1970's, however, climbers from Colorado and elsewhere pushed the new free climbing standards onto the Tower. By the early 1980's dozens of routes up to 5.12 were available for the increasing numbers of climbers. While many thousands of climbers have reached the summit, the great majority still use the **Durrance Route**.

CAMPING

Inside the Monument boundaries and next to the Belle Fourche River, is a campground ($5 per site). Private campgrounds are also available nearby. At the Monument boundary are small grocery stores, showers and laundry. Free camping is difficult to find because camping in the Monument is only allowed inside designated sites, and ranchers are known to not take kindly to trespassers. An entrance fee is charged to enter the National Monument; Golden Eagle passes are accepted.

SEASONS AND WEATHER

Approximate Months	Typical Temperatures High	Low	Likelihood of Precipitation	Frequency of Climbable Days
Nov-Mar	30's +	20's −	low-med	med-low
Apr-May	60's +	40's −	medium	very high
Jun-Aug	90's	50's +	med-low	very high
Sep-Oct	70's −	40's −	low	very high

Comments: By climbing on the shady or sunny side of the Tower, temperatures can usually be kept comfortable the year round.

RESTRICTIONS AND WARNINGS

Registration at the visitor center is required for climbing the Tower. One must sign in both before and after climbing each day. No overnighting is permitted anywhere except in the campground: no summit bivouacs. Although loose rock elsewhere is not normally a problem, the congestion on the South Face (Durrance Route and Meadows Rappel) can make a hard hat worthwhile. No fixed ropes may be left unattended. Lichen on the rock can become very slippery when wet. The South Face can become too hot to touch during mid-day summer heat.

GUIDEBOOKS

A Poorperson's Guidebook: Free Climbs of Devils Tower (revised almost annually) by Dingus McGee and The Last Pioneer Woman. This cheap book is in topo format, but it has no history or first ascent information. Available locally at the Visitor Center or from Dennis Horning, RR 1 Box 88-Y, Custer, SD 57730. A new comprehensive guidebook is expected to be published soon, authored by Richard Guilmette (Chief Ranger) and published by The Mountaineers Books, 306 2nd Avenue West, Seattle, WA 98119.

GUIDE SERVICES AND EQUIPMENT STORES

No services are available locally. The nearest climbing equipment stores are Wheeler Dealer, 425 Gillette Avenue, Gillette, Wyoming; and Mountain Goat Sports, 211 Jackson Boulevard, Rapid City, South Dakota.

EMERGENCY SERVICES

In case of emergency, contact a park ranger—they can coordinate rescues and ambulances. The nearest hospital is twenty-eight miles away: Crook County Memorial Hospital, 7130 AK, Sundance, telephone: 283-3501. A clinic is available ten miles north of the Tower: Hulett Community Clinic, 115 Main Street, Hulett, telephone: 467-5934.

GETTING THERE

Public transportation to the Monument is not available.

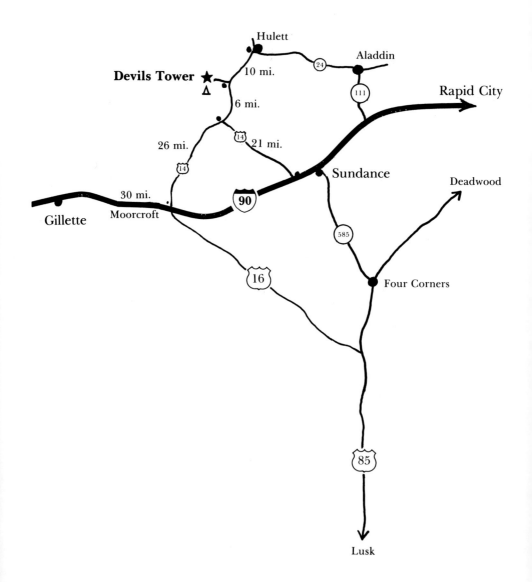

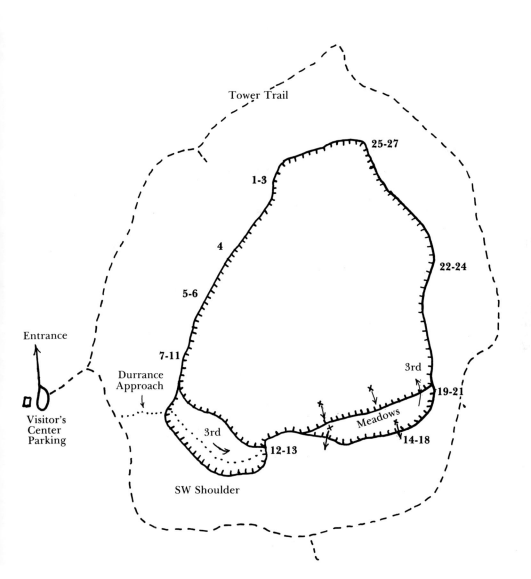

Tower Trail

25-27

1-3

4

5-6

7-11

Entrance

Durrance
Approach

3rd

19-21

3rd

Meadows

14-18

Visitor's
Center
Parking

12-13

22-24

SW Shoulder

West Face

1 **Carol's Crack III 5.11a** Yoho, Chick Holtkamp, Carol Black and Jeff Baird, 1978. Extra medium stoppers.

2 **Approaching Lavender II 5.11c** Paul Piana, Bob Cowan, Todd Skinner and Beth Wald, 1984. Only tiny wires to medium stoppers.

3 **One-Way Sunset III 5.10b** Dennis Horning and Jim Slichter, 1977. Extra small to large stoppers and a couple large nuts to 4+ inches for upper pitches.

4 **Deli Express II 5.12−** Steve Hong and Mark Sonnenfeld, circa 1982. Many tiny stoppers.

5 Bloodguard I 5.12 – Todd Skinner, Beth Wald, Bob Cowan and Paul Piana 1984. Medium stoppers only.

6 Brokedown Palace III 5.12 – Bruce Price and Miles Malone, 1973. FFA: Mark Sonnenfeld and Steve Hong, 1982. Small to medium stoppers.

7 Mr. Clean III 5.11 (or 5.10 C1) Curt Haire and Dennis Horning 1976. FFA: Henry Barber, 1977. Extra medium to large stoppers, a couple large nuts to 4 inches.

8 Tulgey Wood III 5.10a Mark Hesse and Dan McClure, 1972. Extra stoppers all sizes, several 2½ inch to 3½ inch nuts.

West Face

9 McCarthy West Face Variation III 5.10c Chris Ballinger and Dennis Horning, 1978. Extra medium to large stoppers.

10 El Matador III 5.11a Yoho and Chick Holtkamp, 1978. Extra stoppers of all sizes.

11 Digital Extraction II 5.12 − FFA: Steve Hong and Mark Sonnenfeld, circa 1981.

El Matador photo: Dan Hare

South Face

12 **Durrance II 5.7** Jack Durrance and Harrison Butterworth, 1938. The most popular route up the Tower. Large nuts and extra slings.

13 **Weissner II 5.7** Fritz Weissner, William House and Lawrence Coveny, 1937. The first route up the Tower after the cowboy stake ladder. Large nuts and tube chocks.

14 **Bon Homme Variation II 5.8** Dennis Horning and Howard Hauck, 1972. Extra medium to large nuts.

15 **The Power that Preserves II 5.11+** Todd Skinner, 1983. Tiny to medium stoppers.

16 **Direct Southeast II 5.11+** with intermediate belay, 5.12 − without (or 5.5 C2) Pete Ostlund and John Horn, 1965. FFA: Steve Hong, 1978. Many tiny to small stoppers.

17 **Walt Bailey Memorial II 5.9** Gary Cole, Ray Jacquot and Charles Blackmon, 1959. FFA: Scott Woodruff and Jeff Overton, 1974. Extra medium stoppers.

18 **Hollywood and Vine III 5.10c** Ray Jacquot and Gary Cole, 1960. FFA: Scott Woodruff and Jeff Overton, 1974. Extra small nuts.

Durrance Route (above), Pseudowiessner (below)

National Park Service equipment demonstration

East Face

19 Soler II 5.9− Anton Soler, Art Lambeck, Herb Conn and Ray Moore, 1951. FFA: Layton Kor and Raymond Jacquot, 1959. Extra medium nuts.

20 Tad II 5.7 Dale Gallagher and Jack Moorehead, 1956. FFA:Dan Burgette and Charles Bare, 1973. Extra medium to 4 inch nuts.

21 El Cracko Diablo II 5.8 Rod Johnson and Pat Padden, 1973.Extra medium to 4 in. nuts.

22 Casper College III 5.10+ Dud McReynolds, David Sturdevant, Walt Bailey and Bruce Smith, 1956. FFA: Dennis Horning and Jim Beyer, 1977. Extra small to medium stoppers.

23 Burning Daylight III 5.10b Mike Todd and Dennis Horning, 1977. Extra medium stoppers.

North Face

24 Belle Fourche Buttress III 5.10− Don Ryan and Gary Cole, 1961. FFA: Dennis Horning and Dave Rasmussen, 1977. Extra medium stoppers.

25 Patent Pending III 5.8+ Charles Bare and Jim Olsen, 1971. FFA: Bruce Bright and Dennis Drayna, 1972. Extra large nuts to 4 inch, optional tube chocks.

26 Assemblyline III 5.9 Dennis Horning and Judd Jennerjahn, 1975. Extra medium nuts to 3 inches.

27 McCarthy North Face III 5.11b or 5.7 C2 Jim McCarthy and John Rupley, 1957. FFA:Dennis Horning and Frank Sanders, 1978. Extra medium to large stoppers.

Gate Buttress

The Fin and The Thumb

LITTLE COTTONWOOD CANYON

HIGHLIGHTS

Perhaps only Boulder, Colorado, offers more excellent climbing within so few minutes of a major town than Salt Lake City. Quartzite cliffs and alpine granite are found within hiking distance of city limits, but it is the superb and extremely accessible crags of Little Cottonwood Canyon which are the best known and most popular. Just a hop, skip, and several jumps from the road, these glacially scoured granite faces proffer a few cracks and a lot of thin face climbing. Because of a frequent dirth of protection, much of the more difficult climbing is also mentally taxing, but not all routes are runout. Summer temperatures on the south facing climbs of the Canyon tend to be too hot for most climbers.

CLIMBING

Little Cottonwood Canyon's most prominent cliffs line the northern wall of a classic, U-shaped, glacially carved canyon. The glacier may have scraped the rock clean and smooth, but it did not leave the slick, shiny sheen of Tuolumne Meadows rock. Indeed, chickenheads are common on certain sections of cliff, providing welcome rests from thin slab climbing.

While face climbing dominates the routes in the Canyon, cracks are not uncommon and most routes follow a crack for part of their length. On the blank faces, bolt protection is the norm—often very widely spaced, however. Bolts were rarely placed on rappel, and routes where they were have some of the most serious runouts in the Canyon anyway. These notorious characteristics usually only show up on the harder routes. A few short, pure crack routes exist as well, some of them quite vicious in difficulty.

The Gate Buttress is possibly the most climbed rock in Utah. Below the cliff in the trees and out of sight of the road are some fine boulders. This is the climbers' hangout, and is a good place to meet kindred spirits.

Be sure to use the trails that lead to and from climbs. These trails were built and are maintained by climbers in order to preserve the integrity of the hillsides.

ENVIRONMENT

Depending on one's cultural or recreational bent, the Salt Lake City area is best known for its powder skiing—some of the deepest and lightest snow in the world falls here—or as the heart of the Mormon religion. As both a religious and state capital, the Salt Lake Valley was chosen with a great sense of physical beauty: the city abuts the Wasatch Range to the east and the Great Salt Lake to the northwest. A great number of outdoor enthusiasts have found Salt Lake City much to their liking, though they also find a problem common to cities walled off by mountains: frequent intense air pollution.

Little Cottonwood Canyon is just outside the city limits, but is high enough to escape the dirty air. The steeply angled canyon sides, combined with their vast snow accumulations, make the Canyon an avalanche controller's dream; in fact, the road to the ski areas is frequently closed in the winter. In the summer, these cliffs catch intense sunlight while climbers catch suntans and mountain views. Because of its accessibility and recreational values, the Canyon receives more visitors each year than Yellowstone and the Tetons combined.

CLIMBING HISTORY

Within days of declaring the Salt Lake Valley to be their new spiritual home, Brigham Young and a few of his Mormon desciples hiked up nearby Mt. Ensign to get a better view of the valley. Aside from this excursion, the closest that the pioneers came to harvesting the bounty of local rock came when they quarried Little Cottonwood Canyon to build the Mormon Temple.

Almost a century later, in 1958, members of the Wasatch Mountain Club (principally a hiking group) made the first recorded technical climbs in the region. The end of the 1950's saw several excellent routes climbed on the alpine granite of Lone Pine Cirque; then in the early 1960's, attention turned to the preeminently accessible Little Cottonwood Canyon. A group of climbers named themselves the Alpenbock Climbing Club and began actively seeking out the challenges of the Canyon. Soon, several widely travelled climbers stopped by to put up new routes; this, in combination with news of the feats in Yosemite and the Tetons, stimulated locals to rapid exploration and skill development. One of the few who could climb 5.9, and who followed a visiting climber up the first 5.10 in 1964, has since become the mayor of Salt Lake City.

In the mid 1960's, only a very small corp of climbers could do the handful of 5.10's that were being established. Still, perhaps the hardest multi-pitch free route in the country was established in 1965: the **Dorsal Fin**.

Through the late 1960's to early 1970's, little growth in the climbing scene occured. 1975 proved to be a turning point, when a rapidly growing number of climbers repeated the area's hard routes. The first guide book appeared in 1976, followed by a second in 1977; simultaneously came an influx of climbers and a push into 5.11, and in 1980, 5.12. Where before the Canyon had seemed to be gleaned of new route potential, during the 1980's a greater number of routes than ever were made available for the comprehensive 1984 guidebook.

CAMPING

The National Forest Service Tanner's Flat Campground, four miles up the Canyon, is the most attractive campsite during its season of May to October ($4 per site; first come, first served). Camping along the Canyon floor is illegal. Campers can find accomodations with showers and amenities in the KOA at 1400 West North Temple for $10.50 and up (per site). Another possibility is the American Youth Hostel ("Avenues Residential Center") at 107 F Street, two blocks north of South Temple, telephone 363-8137. A young, international crowd can be found here as at most hostels, along with a kitchen and laundry facilities, $8.25 for members, $10.90 non-members. A number of cheap hotels can also be found.

SEASONS AND WEATHER

Approximate Months	Typical Temperatures		Likelihood of Precipitation	Frequency of Climbable Days
	High	Low		
Nov-Mar	20's	0's	med-high	low
Apr-Jun	60's+	40's−	medium	high
Jul-Aug	90's−	50's	low	medium
Sep-Oct	70's−	30's	medium	high

Comments: Considerable snow can fall in early spring or late fall, but sunny weather temperatures will usually be comfortable. The lower rocks can be pleasant even in winter.

RESTRICTIONS AND WARNINGS

Stay on trails leading to and from cliffs. These trails are maintained by climbers and are important for insuring the integrity of the environment. To the west of the Fin lie several rocks on private land. These are owned by the Church of Latter Day Saints (Mormons) who keep vast records in vaults buried within the rock. They can get quite upset with anyone trespassing on their land. Also avoid camping on any other private land in the region. Use existing fire-pits, or better yet, use a stove if picnicking on the valley floor; do not camp there. Observe "no-parking" signs; violators are ticketed and their cars are sometimes towed away.

Utah liquor laws are unusual, including the fact that one must purchase anything more alcoholic than beer from a Utah State Liquor Store. Restaurants can only provide the "set-up": glasses, mixers, corkscrews—for a fee, of course.

GUIDEBOOKS

Wasatch Rock Climbs (1984) by Les Ellison and Brian Smoot. Available at local stores or from the American Alpine Club, 113 East 90th Street, New York, NY 10028.

GUIDE SERVICES AND EQUIPMENT STORES

Local equipment stores include Holubar, 3975 South Wasatch Boulevard; Recreational Equipment Inc., 1122 East Brickyard Road; and Timberline Sports, 3155 Highland Drive. Timberline Sports also hosts a guide service.

EMERGENCY SERVICES

In an emergency, call 911 for help. There are twelve hospitals in the Salt Lake Valley; the closest to the Canyon is: Saint Marks, 1200 East 3900 South, emergency: 268-7129, non-emergency: 268-7074.

GETTING THERE

All major forms of public transportation serve Salt Lake City. Bus service to the cliffs is available for $4 from the airport. One can also connect with the bus at the downtown bus station or several other points.

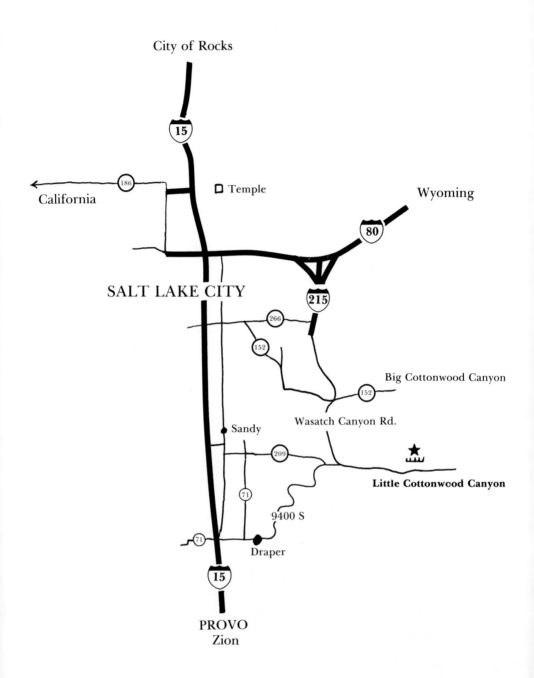

Ted Wilson in Little Cottonwood Canyon photo: Ted Wilson collection

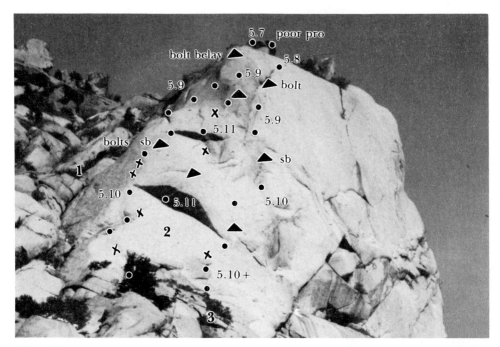

The Fin

Descents, Fin: Bolt rappel north of last belay. Thumb: Rappel into gully east of summit pinnacle, tricky downclimbing below can be bypassed with rap from bolts.

1 **Fin Arete II 5.10** Jonathan and Brian Smoot, 1978. Excellent.

2 **Dark Horse III 5.11** Mark Ward and Kim Miller, 1979. Belay at widely spaced bolts. Serious runout.

3 **The Dorsal Fin III 5.10+** George Lowe and Mark McQuarrie, 1965.

The Thumb

4 **Standard Route with Indecent Exposure . III 5.7** Bob Irvine, Ralph Tingey and Dave Wood, 1962. Caution for rockfall on 1st belay. Pinnacle var.: Robbins Crack 5.10−Royal Robbins and Ted Wilson, 1964.

5 **Spring Fever III 5.10−** Les Ellison and Brian Smoot, 1979. Poor pro.

6 **S Direct III 5.9+** George and Jeff Lowe, 1967. Excellent.

7 **S Crack III 5.8 A2 or 5.11+ A0** Steve Ellsworth, Mark McQuarrie and Ted Wilson, 1964. FFA: George Lowe. var.: **Coyne Crack 5.11+** Leonard Coyne, 1978.

8 **S Matrix III 5.10+** George Lowe, Pete Gibbs and Eric Eliason, 1968. FFA: Brian Smoot and Mark Rolofson, 1979. Poor pro.

9 **Spring and Fall I 5.11** Kim Miller and Mark Ward, 1976.

10 **Monkey Lip I 5.12** Steve Hong and Bob Rotart, 1982.

11 **Robbins Route III 5.10** Royal Robbins and Ted Wilson, 1964. FFA: George Lowe and Eric Eliason.

The Thumb

Gate Buttress

Descent: 2 bolt rappel anchor west of Schoolroom finish.

12 Hatchet Crack 5.7 Bill Conrod and Ed Anderson, 1964.

13 Schoolroom West 5.7 3rd pitch poor pro.

14 Rising Sun 5.11 FFA: Dirk Tyler, 1980.

15 Schoolroom 5.6 Larry Evans, Dick Ream, Rich Ream and Court Richards, 1964. 4 pitches.

16 The Hook 5.8 Fred Becky and Layton Kor, 1961. On 3rd pitch (Hook) lower bolt (below belay bolt) is off route.

17 Bushwack Crack 5.8 Bill Conrod and Paul Anderson.

18 Callitwhatyouplease 5.8 George Lowe and Rich Ream, 1966. Rappel from tree.

The Dihedrals

19 Bitterfingers 5.11+ Merril Bitter, 1981.

20 Hornet's Nest 5.8 Ted Wilson, Rob and Wilf Bruschke.

21 Half a Finger 5.9 Dave Boyd and Eric Eliason, 1970. FFA: Dave Jenkins and Rich W., 1977. Poor pro.

22 Black and White John and Mary 5.10 Dave Boyd and Eric Eliason, 1970. FFA: Les Ellison and Larry Carrol, 1979.

23 Equipment Overhang 5.11− Eric Eliason and Dave Raymond, 1970. FFA: Jack Roberts and Don McCarthy, 1976.

24 Equipment Overhand Right 5.10 FFA: Jack Roberts and Frank Trummel, 1976.

25 Satan's Corner 5.8 Bob Irvine and Dave Wood, 1962. FFA: George Lowe and Ed Anderson.

26 Beckey's Wall 5.7 Fred Beckey and Layton Kor, 1961. Classic.

The view towards Almo.

CITY OF ROCKS

HIGHLIGHTS

The City of Rocks has been designated a National Historic Landmark for its rich Western history, and it could be a Climbing Landmark for the incredible potential of this jungle of rock formations. In the mid 1800's, the California Trail brought up to 50,000 people a year through these rocks; currently it sees limited visitation by either climbers or sightseers, despite the amazing beauty of granite formations that inspire the eye and the muscles. The City lies in the high-desert environment of Southern Idaho and offers comfortable climbing from the spring through the fall. Free camping is available at the cliffs.

CLIMBING

The jumbled chaos of 30-300 foot rocks (most in the 100 foot range) is reminiscent of other desert granite crags like those of Joshua Tree, but the shapes and nature of City crags are considerably more interesting than most. The rock faces are often pock-marked with solution pockets that form by the erosional effects of water seeping through crevices and freezing, expanding and decomposing the underlying rock. The outer skin is especially hard because dissolved minerals solidify near the surface. Thus, the rock is both very solid and very diverse.

Most routes at the City are more likely to follow crack lines than a series of pock-marks. These cracks are often smooth and hard, though rough enough that climbers frequently tape their hands.

The City of Rocks covers an area of about 5,000 acres, with many excellent cliffs scattered well away from dirt roads and rarely visited. Most climbers stick to the rocks near the roads where routes are better known. Even on the more popular cliffs, there is frequently room for new routes; further out, the new route potential is almost unlimited— though rarely is there proof that no one has been there before. In fact, the concensus is to leave first ascent information unrecorded.

Except for Memorial Day Weekend (end of May), the City is little travelled by climbers. The dirt bikers and 4-wheel-drive enthusiasts who have frequently scarred the countryside are, unfortunately, a bit more common on any weekend. Most visitors come from the cities of Boise, Salt Lake, and Jackson.

Many of the rocks are located on private land, behind "No-Trespassing" signs. Among these is the most popular cliff in the City: Elephant Rock. The rock features superb climbing, but routes are not described in this book because of its private status.

ENVIRONMENT

Located at the junction where nearby 10,340 foot Cache Peak rises out of the surrounding high-desert (about 6,000 feet in elevation), the City of Rocks receives more precipitation than the surrounding countryside, and hosts both pine trees and the more prevalent sagebrush-juniper vegetation. Spring is exceptionally beautiful, as flowers from both mountain and desert biomes compete to display their colors.

Despite its National Historic Landmark status—and efforts to have it established as a National Monument—current legal status for the region is so chaotic that little effort is made to curb the off-road vehicle destruction and vandalism that plague the City. Indeed, four-fifths of the land is privately owned by ranchers, while the remaining 1,000 acres is administered by a hodge-podge of governmental agencies, including the Bureau of Land Managment, the U.S. Forest Service, and the Idaho Department of Parks and Recreation. Directions for management are currently being charted, and feedback from environmentally concerned climbers could exert a positive influence: BLM, Burley District Office, Route 3 Box 1, Burley, ID 83318; U.S.F.S., Burley Ranger District, 2621 South Overland, Burley, ID 83318; I.D.P.&R., Statehouse Mail, 2177 Warm Springs Avenue, Boise, ID 83720.

CLIMBING HISTORY

The "Silent City of Rocks" holds a special place in the annals of Western history, as it was the frequent camping place for hundreds of thousands of migrants taking the California Cut-Off from the Oregon Trail. Thousands passed through here each year, admiring the beauty of these rocks and worrying about the possibility (and occasional occurence) of Shoshone Indian ambushes.

Since the advent of the interstate freeway system, people have tended to speed on by, never travelling the forty extra miles and dirt roads to visit the City. Climbers in the know, well-travelled visitors and residents of the cities that lie within a 200 mile radius, have been delighting in the City's wonders since rock climbing became popular in the 1960's.

But the region's climbing history is completely undocumented through deliberate non-reporting by the activists. This lack of information means that climbing here has been especially adventurous for those without knowledge of the routes, and it is felt by many that ratings and names should be left out of the printed literature. However, several guidebooks are currently in the making, though none are widely distributed as yet. Because of the lack of documentation, routes and even rocks can have a multiplicity of names; those listed in this book are among the names in common usage.

By wandering out into the outskirts of the City, one can leave behind both other climbers and any knowledge of route nomenclature—returning to the historical state of climbing at the Silent City of Rocks.

CAMPING

Free camping can be found almost anywhere in the City (avoiding private land), though more developed (BLM) sites and water are found near the Twin Sisters. Free flowing water throughout the City used to offer good drinking, but has become contaminated by human and hoofed traffic. Groceries, gas and other basic supplies can be found during limited hours in Almo. Larger nearby towns, such as Burley, must be visited for showers, hotels, and other amenities.

SEASONS AND WEATHER

Approximate Months	Typical Temperatures High	Low	Likelihood of Precipitation	Frequency of Climbable Days
Nov-Mar	30's +	20's −	med-high	low
Apr-Jun	70's	40's	medium	very high
Jul-Aug	80's +	50's	low	high
Sep-Oct	70's −	40's	medium	high

RESTRICTIONS AND WARNINGS

Much of the City of Rocks is under private ownership.

GUIDEBOOKS
City of Rocks Idaho, A Climber's Guide (1985) by Dave Bingham. Available from various stores or from Dave Bingham, PO Box 1932, Ketchum, ID 83340.

GUIDE SERVICES AND EQUIPMENT STORES
Local services are non-existent, though some guides based out of Salt Lake City and elsewhere may be familiar with the area.

EMERGENCY SERVICES
In case of an emergency, try calling the Cassia County Sheriff at 208-678-2251. A hospital can be found in Burley: Cassia Memorial Hospital, 2303 Park Avenue, telephone: 678-4444.

GETTING THERE
Unless one is willing to endure potentially slow hitch-hiking, a car is necessary to reach the City of Rocks.

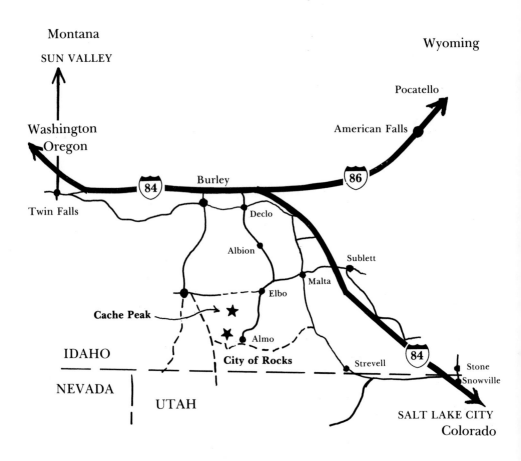

APPROXIMATE DISTANCES:
Burley-City of Rocks, 40 mi.
Salt Lake City-City of Rocks, 150 mi.

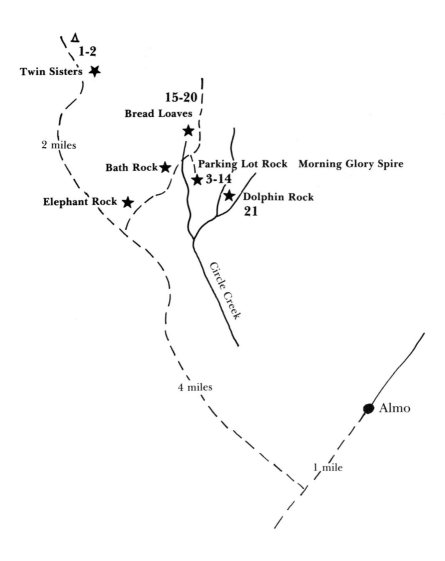

Twin Sisters ★

1-2

15-20

Bread Loaves ★

2 miles

Bath Rock ★

Parking Lot Rock   Morning Glory Spire

★ 3-14

Elephant Rock ★

★ Dolphin Rock

21

Circle Creek

4 miles

● Almo

1 mile

Eberhorn (Higher Sister) photo: Dave Bingham
1 **South Face 5.4** Start in notch.
2 **Eberhorn 5.9** or 5.10 variations

View of Register, Elephant Rocks photo: Dave Bingham

Alan Bard on Elephant Rock photo: Reid Dowdle

Morning Glory Spire
  3 Skyline 5.8
  4 Acceptable Risk 5.10+
  5 Incisor 5.11
  6 Open Door 5.10−

Parking Lot Rock – West Side (Cougar Camp Rock)
  7 Norma's Book 5.5
  8 Batwings 5.8
  9 No Parking 5.10

Parking Lot Rock, East Side
  10 Cougar Face 5.8
  11 Tow-Away Zone 5.9+
  12 5.10+
  13 Stress Fracture 5.10
  14 Thin Slice 5.10

Parking Lot Rock, West Side (Cougar Camp Rock) photo: Dave Bingham

Parking Lot Rock, East Side photo: Dave Bingham

Upper Breadloaves (Slot Machine) photo: Dave Bingham

Dolphin photo: Dave Bingham

Stan Caldwell on Dolfin Dihedral photo: Dave Bingham

Upper Breadloaves
15 Roman Meal 5.8
16 Face and Undercling 5.8
17 5.7
18 Book 5.8
19 Fred Rasmussen 5.8
20 Urban Renewal 5.11

Dolphin
21 Dolphin Dihedral 5.11

Nez Perce Spire

BLODGETT CANYON

HIGHLIGHTS

Western Montana is blanketed by a vast wilderness; forests and mountains stretch from horizon to horizon, with little-known cliffs criss-crossing the hills. Of the many rock climbing areas in this huge state, Blodgett Canyon, in the Bitteroot Mountains, was selected for this book because of its large cliffs, fairly convenient access, and relatively extensive route documentation. One to two hours of hiking lead from the campground to a set of cliffs with both short free routes and Grade V aid climbs. The routes follow good crack systems up steep exfoliated granite that is sometimes glacially polished, sometimes coarse, and occasionally loose. Projecting from the lushly forested hillsides, these white granite shields become solar ovens on a sunny day. Surprisingly, this northern region is not necessarily a haven from midsummer heat, but instead is usually best visited in the spring and fall climbing seasons.

CLIMBING

Because climbing pressure has been very light on Blodgett Canyon's cliffs, only a fraction of the obvious lines have been ascended and some of the aid climbs have seen little serious free climbing effort. This inattention reflects itself even in which cliffs have been climbed. At the mouth of the canyon, near the campground, at least a half-dozen distinct cliffs, averaging about 500 feet in height, line the north wall of the valley. The cliffs that loom over the campground, however, have seen few climbers because the rock is not considered as good as that further up the canyon.

The climbing cliffs up the canyon from the campground are reached by hiking about two miles on a well groomed trail, followed by an energetic hour up loose talus and brush slopes to the cliffs themselves.

The cliffs are not simply cut out of the hillside; instead, they project from the valley's flank and have their own distinct summits, usually in the form of a long arete that connects back to the hillside. Most of the routes are on the south or south-west exposures of these cliffs, making them sometimes excrutiatingly hot on a warm mid-summer's day. Conversely, they offer quite comfortable climbing on a clear day in the spring or fall, even when snow blankets the hillsides.

The major climbing routes ascend the south faces of a series of isolated granite aretes with abundant horns and buttresses. While shorter slabs and buttresses exist below the main faces, Shoshone and Blackfoot Dome are about 500 feet in height, and Nez Perce and Flathead about 1,000 feet.

The granite is reminiscent of fractured alpine rock, though edges are often not as sharp. Because this valley was relatively recently glaciated, the rock is often, though not extensively, polished. Established routes climb the few continuous large corner systems; most new routes will connect the more common shallow, discontinous dihedrals that have resulted from exfoliation. The inside walls of many cracks are smoothly polished ("slickensides").

ENVIRONMENT

Western Montana is comprised of tremendous coniferous forests and little-travelled mountain ranges. The Bitteroot Range is no exception. This 200 mile expanse of mountains rises up to 10,000 feet in height, and numerous glacially carved valleys cut into its eastern flank. Blodgett Canyon's U-shaped valley, with abundant hanging side-valleys, extends twelve miles up to the Idaho-Montana divide in the Selway-Bitteroot Wilderness. This is the second largest wilderness in the continental United States.

Many of the eastern Bitteroot valleys hold granite cliffs and have trails cutting through the dense forests. These trails are commonly used by hikers, professional horse-packers, and hunters, but rarely does one hear the tinkle of climbing hardware. Blodgett Canyon is the principal exception, and weekends often see climbers from Missoula plying its trails and cliffs.

The campground, set amid 100 foot fir trees and with dense under-growth and a clear, full stream rushing by, is more reminiscent of the Pacific Northwest than of the other climbing areas covered in this book. The altitude along the valley floor, about 4,000 feet, is also lower than that found in the southern Rockies.

CLIMBING HISTORY

Blodgett Canyon's climbing history is brief and simple. Though the peaks deeper in the Bitteroots had been explored by technical climbers years before, it was not until 1971 that the first serious route was established in Blodgett—a Grade V ascent of the **South Face of Flathead**. However, this climb was still an isolated incident, for it was not until later in the 1970's that Missoula rock climbers began frequenting the canyon more regularly.

By the 1980's, a small group of students from the University of Montana (in Missoula) were casually developing Blodgett and other more remote cliffs, and informal photocopy guides circulated among the tiny climbing community. With no competition for new routes or first free ascents, climbing in this region has grown slowly in a relaxed, non-pressured environment.

CAMPING

The small Forest Service campground at the head of the road is convenient for car campers, is beautiful in its views of cliffs and trees, is usually uncrowded, offers a plentiful supply of firewood—and is free. There is also a fun bouldering rock within the campground. The only problem is a lack of safe drinking water; water from the nearby stream should be purified. Another inconvenience is occasional noisy weekend parties by Hamilton High School students. All the usual city amenities can be found in Hamilton, six miles from the campsite.

SEASONS AND WEATHER

Approximate Months	Typical Temperatures· High	Low	Likelihood of Precipitation	Frequency of Climbable Days
Nov-Mar	30's+	10's	high	low-med
Apr-Jun	60's	40's	med-high	high-med
Jul-Aug	80's+	50's	low-med	high
Sep-Oct	60's+	40's −	med-low	high

Comments: Because the cliffs face south, sunny-day temperatures can be much higher than the ambient air temperature.

RESTRICTIONS AND WARNINGS

From April to June, there is a tremendous concentration of wood ticks. The Center for Rocky Mountain Spotted Fever is located in Hamilton for this reason (the disease is seriously debilitating and is carried by ticks). Careful inspection, several times per day, is needed to prevent the ticks attaching themselves to the skin. Blodgett Canyon is not remote from a town, but that town has no climbing rescue facilites; cautious climbing ensures survival.

GUIDEBOOKS

No official guidebook exists. At times, the Trailhead in Missoula and the University of Montana Outdoor Recreation Department have carried copies of an informal photocopy guide by Marvin McDonald (1982).

GUIDE SERVICES AND EQUIPMENT STORES

Several stores in Missoula (fifty miles north) sell climbing gear, including High Country in the Southgate Mall on Hwy 93 South, the Army Navy Economy Store at 322 North Higgins Avenue, and the Trailhead at Higgins and South 3rd West. In Hamilton, Mountain Outfitters Supply at 200 Main has sold some climbing gear in the past and may continue to do so. No local guide services exist.

EMERGENCY SERVICES

In case of emergency, call the Ravalli County Sheriff (and ambulance) at 363-3033. The nearest hospital is in Hamilton: the Marcus Daly Memorial Hospital Corp., 1200 Westwood Drive, telephone: 363-2211. "Lifeflight" helicopter-ambulance service from St. Patrick's Hospital in Missoula can be summoned by 911 emergency or 721-9669 direct line to the hospital. The patient is charged $6.66 per air mile (about $700 for Blodgett).

GETTING THERE

Greyhound buses serve Hamilton, six miles from Blodgett Canyon. Hitch-hiking to the campground may be feasible on weekends. Regularly scheduled airline flights serve Missoula, and a tiny airport also exists in Hamilton. From either place, a car can be rented.

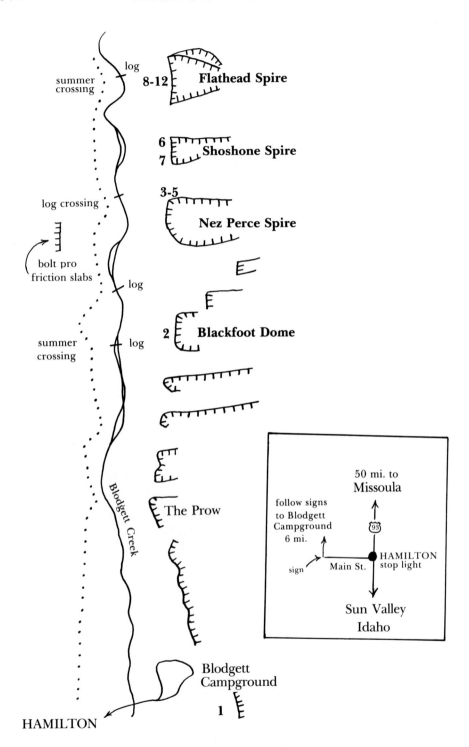

summer crossing

log

8-12   **Flathead Spire**

6
7   **Shoshone Spire**

log crossing

3-5

Nez Perce Spire

bolt pro friction slabs

log

2   **Blackfoot Dome**

summer crossing   log

Blodgett Creek

The Prow

50 mi. to
Missoula

follow signs to Blodgett Campground 6 mi.

93

HAMILTON
stop light

sign   Main St.

**Sun Valley
Idaho**

Blodgett
Campground

1

HAMILTON

Ann Hayes rappelling the Afterburner

Campground Cliffs
1 Bolts to Nowhere 5.9 A2 Sam Braxton and Ray Breuninger. Unfinished route, perhaps just put up for testing bolts.

Blackfoot Dome
2 The Free Lament III 5.9+ or 5.9 A3 Tobin Kelly and Marvin McDonald. FFA: Bill Dockins and Kim Keeting, about 1981. Free ascent involves poor protection. Bring several each: KB, LA (long thick and short thin), hooks, RURPs.

Colby Katchmar and Doug Colwell on Marvin's Wall photo: Kurt Kleiner

West Face Nez Perce Spire

Descent: Hike north along ridge until it is possible to scramble down east into gully between Nez Perce and Blackfoot Dome.

3 **Marvin's Wall V 5.9 A3** Kurt Kleiner, Doug Colwell and Colby Katchmar, 1982. Bring nuts to 3½", 10 KB, 15 LA, 3 ea. ½"-¾", 2 ea. 1"-1½", hooks.

4 **Direct Start 5.9 A2** Mike Scott and Kevin Green, 1983.

5 **Southwest Buttress IV 5.9** Greg Lee and Tom Shreve. Many variations are possible.

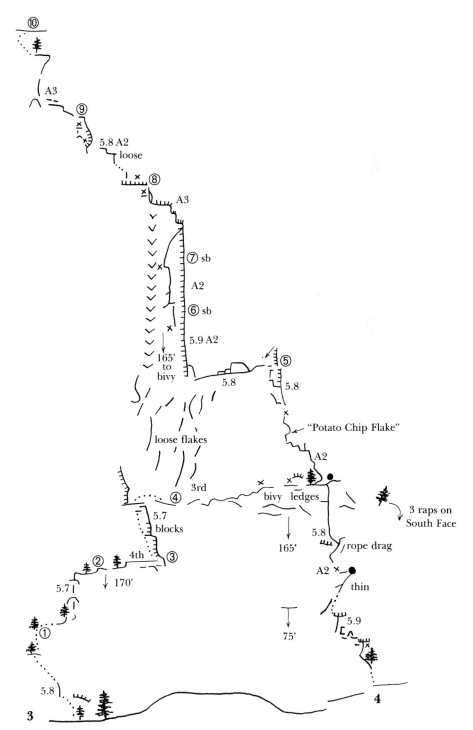

Nez Perce – West Face

Tobin Kelly on Fresh Aire photo: Kurt Kleiner

Shoshone Spire

Descent: Hike north about 100 yards, then turn into gully to the east. Make one 150 foot rappel from fixed slings on large pine tree to within a few yards of the base of the waterfall between Shoshone and Nez Perce. Two ropes are needed for the rappel; one can be left near the start of the climb and picked up on the descent.

  6 South Face Standard Route II-III 5.8 Al Day and Ray Breuninger, about 1970. The lower pitches are optional. Many variations possible.

  7 In Memoriam III 5.10 Elliot Dubriel and Steve Eddy, 1975.

Flathead Spire (Above and left is Beaverhead Buttress)

Descent: 5 rappels from trees down East Face or walk north up ridge ½ mile, then walk east down grassy slabs.

8 **Southwest Buttress III 5.10** FFA: Tom Ballard, Marvin McDonald and Paul Beaufait. Many variations possible.

9 **Fresh Aire V 5.10 A3+** Marvin McDonald, Tobin Kelly and Kurt Kleiner, 1980. Bring complete aid rack, including copperheads, rurps, bathooks and hooks.

10 **My Mom's Muscle Shirt (South Face) V 5.10+ or 5.8 C2** Tom Ballard and Mark Everingham, 1971. FFA: Alex Lowe and Tom Ballard, 1979. Tube chocks can be useful.

11 **The Afterburner II 5.10−** Alex Lowe and Marvin McDonald, 1978.

12 **Tango Tower II 5.9** Alex Lowe and Marvin McDonald, 1978. Tube chocks helpful.

Flathead Spire – Southwest Buttress

Flathead Spire – South Face

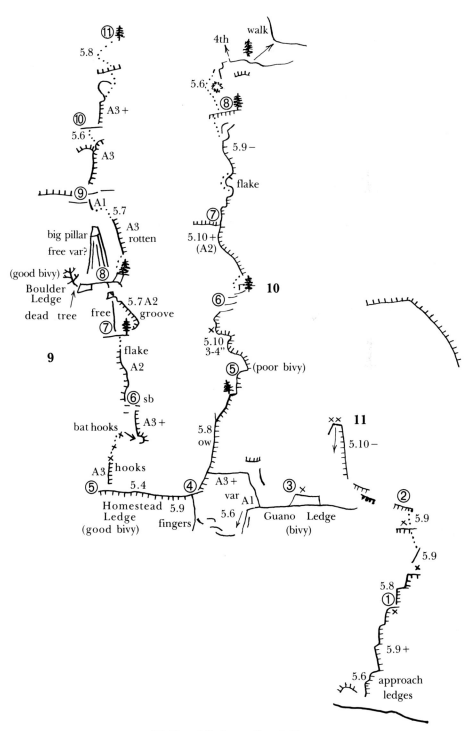

Flathead Spire – South Face

INDEX

(Route Information)

THE AUTHOR:
Although born in California, John Harlin's early years were spent in the Alps—where his father climbed and his mother taught science. After his father's death on the Eiger in 1966, the family returned to America. During his teenage years, John spent as much time as possible in the wilderness, including several month long hiking and kayaking trips to the North Slope of Alaska. But climbing did not become a serious passion for him until his enrollment at the University of California, Santa Barbara, for a degree in Environmental Biology. Since then, he has climbed in numerous rock and mountain centers throughout North America and Europe. Besides writing, John shares his love of the mountain environment through guiding and lecturing.

THE ILLUSTRATOR:
A native of Colorado, Adele Hammond received her undergraduate art training at the College of Creative Studies, University of California, and her MFA from the School of Visual Arts in New York. She is a professional fine artist who makes colorful, interpretive paintings and pastels. Her art has little in common with the illustrations in this book, except that it shows a similar love of nature.